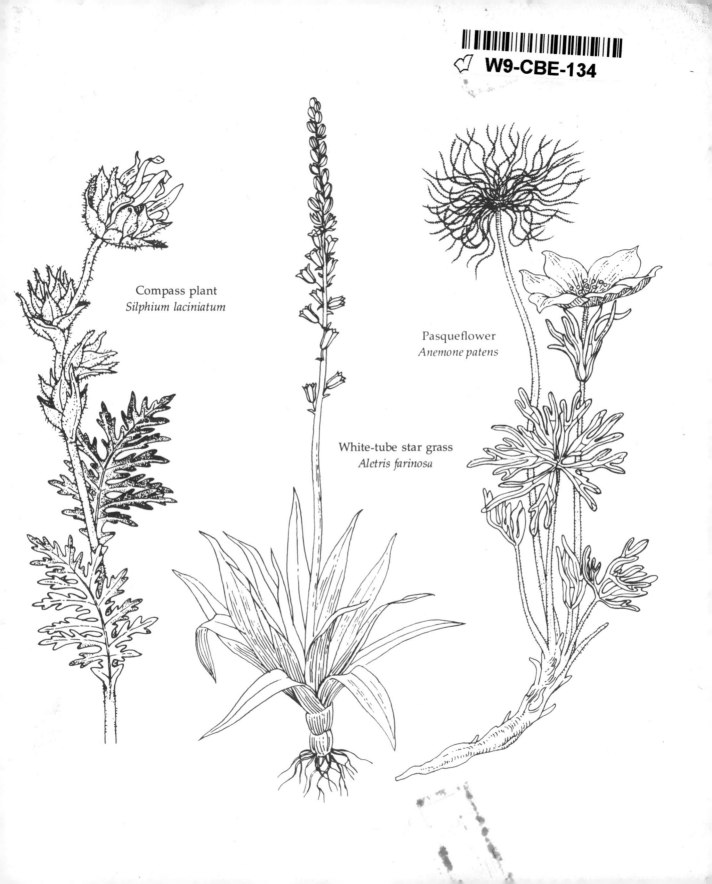

Compass plant
Silphium laciniatum

White-tube star grass
Aletris farinosa

Pasqueflower
Anemone patens

PLANT MEDICINE
AND FOLKLORE

PLANT MEDICINE AND FOLKLORE

MILDRED FIELDER

With photographs by the author
and line drawings by Juan C. Barberis

WINCHESTER PRESS

Copyright © 1975 by Mildred Fielder

Library of Congress Catalog Card Number: 75–9262
ISBN: 0–87691–205–6

Library of Congress Cataloging in Publication Data

Fielder, Mildred.
Plant medicine and folklore.

Bibliography p. 249
Includes index.
1. Botany, Medical—United States.
2. Materia Medica, Vegetable—United States.
3. Indians of North America—Medicine.
I. Title.
QK99.U6F5   581.6'34'0973   75–9262
ISBN 0–87691–205–6

Designed by M. F. Gazze Nimeck

Published by Winchester Press
205 E. 42nd St., New York, N.Y. 10017

Printed in the United States of America

ACKNOWLEDGMENTS

An acknowledgment of appreciation is made to *Twelve/Fifteen* for "This One is Good, This One is Poison," May 1962; to *Bits and Pieces* for "Nervousness and Bad Dreams," May 1965; and to *Caravel* for "Cattail," first quarter, 1958.

Permissions to quote stated excerpts have been given by Dodd, Mead & Company (Reprinted by permission of Dodd, Mead & Company from *A Pocket Guide to the Trees*, by Rutherford Platt. Copyright 1952 by Rutherford Platt); by *Frontiers*, Academy of Natural Sciencee' Philadelphia, for a quotation from an article by J. Almus Russell, "Doctoring with Herbs," February 1957; and by J. B. Lippincott Company for a quotation from *The Eyes of Discovery*, by John Bakeless, 1950.

To the members of the Homestake Library, Lead, South Dakota, and particularly to Dorette Darling, we wish to admit that without their patience and interest in securing source material that sometimes required months to find, we could not have successfully achieved this book.

CONTENTS

PREFACE

Once human beings lived in wilderness areas and used the wild plants found growing there. It seems only common sense that today the average person, you and I, should be able to recognize useful plants and separate them from the worthless plants even as our forefathers did. If in the process of reading about them you might also be entertained, so much the better.

Because we must accept one authority for scientific botanical names to avoid what might become utter confusion, we have used *Gray's Manual of Botany*, edited by Merritt L. Fernald, 8th edition (New York: American Book Company, 1950), to modernize the ethnobotanical names found in many sources. Photo identification has been aided primarily by the excellent descriptions and illustrations in Henry A. Gleason, *The New Britton and Brown Illustrated Flora of the United States and Canada* (Lancaster, Pa.: Lancaster Press, 1952).

Though all of the books listed in the bibliography were consulted at one time or another in compiling this book, we are particularly indebted to the reports of Melvin R. Gilmore and his research on the plants used by the Indians of the Missouri River basin, and to Huron H. Smith for his research on the Indians of Wisconsin.

Since this is a folklore book written for its historical and entertainment value, we have included many popular or familiar names for the various plants as we were able to find them with any degree of accuracy. While Britton and Brown's common names (*Illustrated Flora of the Northern United States, Canada and the British Possessions*, New York: Charles Scribner's Sons, 1913) have been of great help, other historical and botanical sources were consulted as well. For spellings, we have relied chiefly on *Webster's Third New International Dictionary*. The common names of wild plants overlap with such consistent inconsistency that we must after all fall back on the botanical names for final reference, and those who want to find these plants are urged to do so with the botanical names foremost in mind.

Honeysuckle can be any of several plants, skunkweed has been applied to various plants that smell bad, windflower can refer to several unrelated flowers. Even odd names like poverty weed can mean more than one flower. For this reason, we urge you to check all references pertaining to the one you may be searching to get the whole picture. Lists of common names for each plant are not always repeated, usually being included only once. If you know a familiar name for the plant in question, by following through on all references to its Latin name, obtained by trial-and-error reference, you can ultimately find the full information you may want.

One caution is necessary for the casual reader. In discussing these various plants and their uses for foods or medicines, we are tempted to try them ourselves. Before doing so, it is necessary to check Walter C. Muenscher's *Poisonous Plants of the United States* (New York: Macmillan, 1939), which lists some 1,600 plants. Some plants previously gathered for foods can become dangerous if they are fertilized with modern chemicals. Many plants considered medically valuable on the frontier are listed as poisonous today, perhaps their inherent poison being what influenced their acceptance as medicine. We report them as folklore and for their historical interest. Do not use them haphazardly if you value your health. —M.F.

PLANT MEDICINE AND FOLKLORE

CATTAIL

The marsh held thickened mud beneath the ooze,
and water stained with dust along the top.
The sun was high and hot. We felt the cool
of swampy liquid blandishing our feet
and laughed with joy. The cattails swung beyond
our grasp, erect and stately tall. Their heads
were cylinders of firmness fuzzy tailed
to hide their wealth. We knew their secret well.

We gathered cattails all that day, a pile
that grew along the bank like cobs of corn,
and left no single spike. When all was done,
the marsh was green with leaves but brown was stripped
from every crusty stalk. And then, because
we both were young—we two who lived when time
began—we each took one and broke its heart
to spread its softness on our prescient palms.

The flocculus meant blessings for our tribe
and many others. When a babe was born
he first was laid within the cattail down.
When stones about the fireplace burned our hands
or scalding liquid spilled upon bare toes
our mothers spread the soothing cattail there
and pain was eased. How many bouncing babes
had ridden in their mothers' cradles strapped
upon her back? So many ones had known
the comfort of the padded cattail fluff
against their skin.

   We stroked its earthy white
of cushioned typha latifolia
and liked the touch. We smiled. The sun hung low
and time was calling. Gather all the cobs
of brown, archaic sprites, and hie for home.
The smoke of fires lifts lazy from the hill.

INTRODUCTION: NO DOCTOR? WHAT SHALL WE DO?

*T*here is nothing more deeply entrenched in American folklore than a belief in the medicinal virtues of wild plants. When the explorers of the great Western plains and mountains first went up the rivers, they found primitive American Indians with full knowledge of what plants were valuable for various ailments. Whether early settlers gained this information from the plains Indians or whether they came from earlier frontiers with that familiarity of plants is a question that is hard to answer. Certainly the settlers used wild plants as remedies, too, and the practice does not stop with them.

If we take a wild leap into the present century we can find living persons who will tell us, "Yes, I have tasted pennyroyal tea. My mother always gave it to us to throw off a cold." Or they will refer to plantain, or pleurisy root, or a cup of mint tea, with magnificent unconcern as they would speak of any accepted remedy.

Suppose we make no direct attempt to evaluate the healing properties of such plants, but look at them only as folklore. If we consider them with an open mind, they tell us much of the

1

early life of American frontiers that we would not otherwise know.

The first thing that comes to our attention is that the Indians before the time of white man's coming were just as humanly open to suffering and pain as the most educated white or red man today. The settler and the wild plains redman were brothers under the skin. Though they spoke a different language at first, it was not long before they knew that they thought alike. A headache in one was just as painful as a headache in the other. Poison ivy could cause as much distress to a dark skin as to a light one. One stomach could contract with inner pain just as miserably as another stomach. The pure revealing answer was that what cured a person with one background would cure another with quite a different background.

Names of illnesses today have become rather more illuminating than they were in frontier days. When the land was young and people had to depend on their own resources, they did not have the medical knowledge to say they were suffering an attack of polio or impetigo or virus pneumonia, but they certainly knew the symptoms of what ailed them. They had boils on their skin, bowels which cramped and ran, burns from scalding water and hot stones. Despite the myth that Indian women had their babies with no trouble whatsoever, there were plenty of complications in childbirth. Colds were rampant, as one might easily suppose when one studies the flimsy homes and inadequate clothing of some of the uncivilized tribes.

Colic, or gas on the stomach, was far from unknown. Some historians mention plants taken for fainting or convulsions. Earache and eye trouble were common. Fever was a frequent symptom; the list of plants to combat it is long. Some plants were only a general tonic to build one up in the springtime, or taken simply because "it's good for you." Others had value in reducing swelling in glands such as occurs in mumps.

There were headaches, kidney trouble, lung trouble, sores in the mouth, heart ailments. We do not wonder that early Americans were also victims of nervousness and bad dreams. Neuralgia or rheumatism or various unnamed aches and pains were common. Nosebleed had its special remedies. Skin eruptions, abrasions, and infections were treated by a variety of plants. Even snakebite and spider bite called for specialized treatment. Toothache? Oh, yes, and no dentists to care for them. Even, we regret to say, worms in the intestinal tract.

Lastly and perhaps very important, there were wounds, for both settlers and Indians; the frontier was rough country for one and a land of fighting and hunting for both. There may have been many more plants that were found to stanch the blood and heal the cuts of the fighting men, but histories have given us plenty that can be directly traced to such needs.

In a discussion of early medical plants, it seems easier to take them in regard to the illness for which they were known. We must emphasize that we are not advocating going into the woods and the prairies to find these plants for that specific remedy. We have not tried them ourselves, and we speak of them only from their folklore interest. Again we warn, too, that some plants accepted medically by Indians or frontiersmen are recognized as poisonous today. The mere fact of their toxicity may have been why they were used as medicine—they produced visible physical effects on the patient.

Whether that was good or bad has little to do with our purpose of reporting medical plant folklore, but it should be a caution to the reader. Do not try these recipes unless you are willing to take chances with your life—and perhaps also with the law, for many wild plants are protected by state laws, and many more should be.

Of course we tend to distrust such remedies anyway. We read of ancient medicine men, witch doctors, old crones with their brewing pots. The descriptions surrounding such practitioners are usually so graphic and entrancing that we are tempted to assume that most of their alleged healing powers must have come from some source of hypnotic persuasion. Yet as we look at these old plants, we begin to wonder. Many of them have basic ingredients that are in scientific preparations today. The wild licorice, for instance, reminds us that today licorice in commercial quantities is in cough drops and cough remedies.

Modern pharmaceutical books list many of the early plant medicines as part of twentieth-century prescriptions. Joseph P. Remington's *The Practice of Pharmacy*, published in 1917, lists at

3

least 110 plant sources whose names one recognizes from the primitive or frontier medicine man's cures. Obviously there was some definite basis to the beliefs held by Indians and white settlers in a day when there was no doctor on the other end of a telephone. They had to do something. Somehow, they managed to find the right medicines in the fields and forests.

We cannot possibly have found all the plants that belong in folklore. We have mentioned as many as could be checked by accepted authorities, but there are others tucked away in grandmother's memory. Many more may be forgotten for the time. They'll come back. All of our wild plants have some value, though we may not recognize it when we look at them. In these days of chemical weed control, we who see more in the wild growing green than the term "weeds" are inclined to shudder at their wholesale slaughter.

An Associated Press dispatch in June 1954 listed the uses being made by a Syracuse University research team of the common cattail. During World War II the cattail down stuffed lifejackets, baseballs, and mattresses, just as the Indians stuffed cradle boards and pillows with it. The roots can be eaten as vegetables or ground into an edible flour. The stems have long been adapted to calk the ends of barrels. The cattail fibers, the seeds, the sticky substance in the stem are all valuable.

Many common foods and spices were thought to have medicinal value—and perhaps some of them do. The frontier prescription of onions for colds is interesting in the light of recent research. In 1947, a paper was presented to the American Chemical Society in which Edward F. Kohman reviewed certain experiments made with onions. He described the curative effect of onion vapors upon purulent inflammatory wounds, and the bactericidal properties of raw onions when chewed upon the lining of the mouth. He suggests that there is a sound basis for some of the old beliefs concerning the healing properties of the onion from his own experiments with their bactericidal and phytoncidal properties. Maybe our grandmothers were not being foolish when they placed a pan of sliced onions under a sick person's bed.

Mint? Maybe we don't confine ourselves just to the *Mentha arvensis* varieties that grow wild over the northern plains states, but there are many mints gathered today. Oil of the mints are flavorings for cooking, in medicines, perfumes, dental preparations, chewing gums, fruit drinks, teas, vinegars, jellies, soups, sauces, and liqueurs. We have not forgotten the mint.

Mustard? Enough said.

Sage? There is some in the cupboard. Chokecherries? These black fruits are found throughout the West in great quantity. Many modern homes have found that chokecherry jelly is a tasty dish to set on the table. No one makes any rash statements about chokecherry jelly being a cure for dysentery or diarrhea, but if it is, who will object?

You can buy hibiscus tea, rose-hip tea, mint tea, elderberry and black-currant teas in some specialty shops. In Southern desert towns you might find cactus jelly on the shelves.

Wild plums? Pin cherries? Grapes? They all grow today, and they are gathered by anyone who knows them for their food value.

Drugs are derived from many of the early medicinal plants, and made available in druggists' shops today. Fluid of *Grindelia* is one of many still available. Some of the plants known as poisonous, such as monkshood, yield drugs for modern medicines.

One cannot list in a brief survey all the ways that we have benefited from plant folklore. Research continues on many wild plants, and it is possible that valid reasons will be found for many of the old magics and cures.

No . . . the old ways are not gone entirely.

BITES, WOUNDS, AND PARASITES

BITES

*W*e find references to snakebite remedies in the earliest of explorer's histories. Maximilian, Prince of Wied, wrote in his chronicle of his trip up the Missouri River in 1833 of several snakebite remedies:

. . . lion's heart [*Prenanthes rubicunda*] is commended as a sovereign remedy against the bite of serpents. Old Dutot related a number of successful cures which he had performed with this root. This plant has a tall flower stem with many flowers, and large arrow shaped leaves; its root is partly tuberous, partly long, pretty large, and branching, of a reddish yellow colour, and contains a milky juice. It is boiled with milk, and two table-spoonfuls are taken as a dose. The swelling, caused by the bite of the reptile, is said speedily to disappear, after chewing the root.[1]

He related somewhat later in his narration that

One of the sons of Mr. Sachs, our landlord, has been lately bitten by a rattlesnake while fishing, and they affirmed that he was soon cured by

[1]Maximilian, Prince of Wied, *Travels in the Interior of North America*. Reprinted by Thwaites, Reuben Gold, in *Early Western Travels*. Cleveland: Arthur H. Clark Co., 1906. Vol. 1, p. 95.

tea made of the bark of the white ash, which is said to be an infallible antidote to the bite of serpents.[2]

An old history of frontier Illinois, *Recollections of the Pioneers of Lee County*, bears up Maximilian's dosage of snakeroot and milk. One of the teachers in the early 1830s tells how she dealt with an emergency snakebite. First she whipped the snake to death with a long switch, she says, then took care of her pupil.

Andrew Bainter tied his whip-lash tightly around the leg, just above the wound. I soon found some Seneca snake root, and gathering a quantity, bruised some between two stones and bound it with my handkerchief on to the wounded foot and took him, with a quantity of the snake-root, home to his mother, instructing her to steep some of it in milk and give him to drink, and to bind some fresh root on the wound, which she did; and much to my surprise and satisfaction the next morning he came to school just a little lame, and soon recovered entirely. What a blessed Providence to provide an antidote for that deadly poison within our reach: and thanks to my mother's instructions, I knew just what to do.[3]

This sounds very interesting, but we have a somewhat let-down feeling when we also read that many snake remedies come from the fact that the root or the leaf or the blossom reminded a person of the appearance of a snake's head, just as plants having a resemblance in their seeds to the shape of a man's liver were said to be thus good for the liver. Maybe the snake in the anecdote was not a poisonous snake, too.

Maximilian's "lion's heart" was a red rattlesnake root. The *Prenanthes* plants are the rattlesnake roots. This tall small-flowered weed still flourishes in open woods over the midland grass states and the Southern states. *P. alba* is the white rattlesnake root once prepared in Midwestern states by steeping the leaves in hot water, then placing them as a poultice on the snakebite. Perhaps your grandmother called it the lion's foot, white cankerweed, milkweed, joy leaf, cancerweed, white lettuce, or wild lettuce.

The root of the silverleaf scurf pea, *Psoralea argophylla*, was another snakebite remedy.

[2]Maximilian, *Travels*, Vol. 1, p. 101.
[3]Lee County Columbian Club, *Recollections of the Pioneers of Lee County*. Dixon, Illinois: Inez A. Kennedy, 1893. P. 95.

Seneca snakeroot
Polygala seneca

Maximilian's white ash, *Fraxinus americana*, is more difficult to pin down as a snake remedy. We know that Indians believed the ash to have mystic powers against the snake as a preventive ingredient keeping the snakes from biting, but we have not found the recipe for how the ash treated a bite, once that occurred.

What about that Seneca snakeroot? It sounds mighty powerful. It seems to be a case of colloquialism taking over two words that were associated. The name "Seneca" is correctly applied to a tribe of early Iroquoian Indians in eastern North America who used the plant, but the root to which we refer is correctly spelled "senega root," or *Polygala senega*. You will find it listed as "Seneca root" as often as "senega root," though, and we will not attempt to arbitrate the spelling. This is one of the milkworts, and contains an irritating soapy substance. The name "milkwort" comes from the original Greek from which its scientific name is composed, which means "much milk" from its supposed virtue as pasturage. In contrast, a more popular family name is the candyroot, which describes the wintergreen flavor of the roots. *P. senega*, Seneca snakeroot, grows in the Black Hills of South Dakota among other places. Search in the deep rocky valleys. Sometimes the plant was combined with the root of wild indigo, *Baptisia leucantha*, for a more effective snakebite remedy. The *Baptisia* is also called white wild indigo and white or prairie false indigo.

The root of plantainleaf sedge, *Carex plantaginea*, was chewed by Indian medicine men of a century ago, then sprayed into a snakebite wound as a cure.

Another old flower book printed in 1866 lists the cohosh bugbane, *Cimicifuga racemosa*, as the black snakeroot or black cohosh, and notes that its root has a reputation as a snakebite antidote. It is a tall flower growing from four to eight feet, with large sharp-toothed leaves and small white flowers in slender spikes, a beautiful giant no matter what century it lives in. It is more easily recognized by the name "fairy candles" for its white flowered spikes, rank-scented though they may be. Other names for it are rich weed, rattleweed, rattlesnake root, rattle-top, and rattleroot.

The root tubers of the tall gayfeather, *Liatris scariosa*, were thought to be a cure for the bite of rattlesnakes. This colorful spike, called colicroot, rattlesnake master, blazing star, rough spike gayfeather, and button snakeroot, likes to grow in sandy soils.

Another completely different plant is called button snakeroot, and should not be confused with *Liatris*. The name "button snakeroot" has become far more the property of *Eryngium aquaticum*, a plant that grows from two to six feet high. Known as button snakeroot eryngo, eryngo, water eryngo, corn snakeroot, rattlesnake master, rattlesnake weed, and rattlesnake flag, the leaves and fruit were part of the Indian medicine men's song-and-dance performed to cure rattlesnake bite. The root of *Eryngium* made a brew taken internally to counteract rattlesnake poison and other poisons.

Gayfeather
Liatris ligulistylis,
very similar to *L. scariosa*
(photograph: Marjorie Morcom)

9

Jack-in-the-pulpit
Arisaema triphyllum

Rippleseed plantain
Plantago major

Wood lily
Lilium philadelphicum

The root of the jack-in-the-pulpit, *Arisaema triphyllum*, was pounded to reduce swelling from a rattlesnake bite.

Although white people seldom considered boneset, *Eupatorium perfoliatum*, for snakebite, some Indian tribes called the plant "snakeroot" and believed that the root cured a person bitten by any snake.

The recommended treatment for a water-moccasin bite was to boil a root of the giant St.-John's-wort, *Hypericum pyramidatum*, dry it, pulverize it to powder, and dust the root powder upon the bite to draw the poison and heal the wound.

Sanicula species are called "snakeroot" as one of their common names, though all may not have been accepted for a venom antidote. The black sanicle or black snakeroot, *Sanicula*

11

Eastern black walnut
Juglans nigra

marilandica, was one that was. Its roots were pounded and made into a poultice, particularly against rattlesnake venom.

The root of common horse gentian, *Triosteum perfoliatum*, was another poultice. This was known by many names — tinker's weed, feverwort, feverroot, wild ipecac, wood ipecac, wild coffee, and genson.

Two flowers recommended for snakebite or spider bite have their interest today because of their showy flowers. The purple coneflower, *Echinacea angustifolia*, *E. pallida*, and *E. purpurea*, claims an antidote for snakebite, and a plant mentioned specifically for spider bite is the gorgeously flamboyant wood lily, the western orangecup lily, *Lilium philadelphicum*. Other names for this forest exotic are the red lily, western red lily, spring

lily, tiger lily, and snake lily. It was chewed and pulverized
and the flower paste applied over the bite. It is too beautiful for
medicine, and too rare a flower. Leave it alone and forget
about any spider bite.

Western yarrow leaves were a poultice for spider bites too.
Sometimes called woolly yarrow, *Achillea lanulosa*, it differs
from the common yarrow in its whiter, downier appearance.

A strange remedy for snakebite is that made from the black
walnut, *Juglans nigra*. Take the twig bark, coil it, char it, and
apply the charred bark in water to the snakebite.

Rippleseed plantain, *Plantago major*, was supposed to protect
you from snakebite if you carried a piece of the root in your
pocket, but if you were bitten anyway you could make a tea of
the plantain leaves to cure the bite.

The root of the Andrews gentian, *Gentiana andrewsii*, was
gathered as an antivenin. This is a blue blossom otherwise
called closed gentian, blind gentian, cloistered heart, bottle
gentian, and barrel gentian. There may have been many more
plants reputed to be snakebite remedies. Were they, or were
they not? Few of us would be tempted to solicit a rattlesnake
bite just to test their power.

If you want to make a particularly good smudge to drive away
mosquitoes, burn some leaves of St. Louis sagebrush or white
sage, *Artemisia ludoviciana*. If they bite anyway, everybody
knows that witch hazel is good for mosquito bites. The witch
hazel shrub, *Hamamelis virginiana*, has been popularly called
the snapping hazel, winterbloom, or wych hazel. In North
Carolina especially, the leaf of the dangerous jimson-weed,
Datura stramonium, was applied on mosquito bites to lessen
the swelling.

Bee stings can be soothed by heated plantain leaves applied
over the wound. Find either the rippleseed plantain, *Plantago
major*, or blackseed plantain, *P. rugelii*. They can be treated also
by a lotion made from the flowers of the stiff goldenrod,
Solidago rigida.

Dog bite could be poulticed by the root of bluebead lily, *Clintonia
borealis*, if you are so unfortunate as to be bitten by man's best
friend. The bluebead lily is recognized by other names—yellow

13

Lichen
Parmelia sp.

Jimsonweed
Datura stramonium

Virginia mountain mint
Pycnanthemum virginianum

clintonia, Clinton's lily, bear tongue, cow tongue, and dog-berry.

The Sioux Indians believed the freshly scraped root of the black sampson or purple coneflower, *Echinacea angustifolia*, could be applied as a poultice against hydrophobia caused by dog bite or other animal bites. In contrast, white settlers once used the slender Virginia mountain mint, *Pycnanthemum virginianum*. It is said that in the Middle Ages a bite from a mad dog was treated by a poultice of lichen and black pepper mixed with warm milk. The lichen could be one of several species. But it is doubtful whether any of these poultices did much good in preventing rabies.

15

Larkspur
Delphinium bicolor

A particularly nasty bite is that made by lice in the hair, a situation by no means unknown to the primitive Indians on the plains as well as to other people. They washed the hair with a bark infusion made from white ash, *Fraxinus americana*. If it was good enough for snakebite it ought to be good enough for lice.

They said, too, that if you dried the seeds of larkspur, *Delphinium consolida* and *D. ajacis* in particular, then made an ointment, a lotion, or a tincture from those dried seeds, you could apply the mixture to destroy lice or the itch mite. The larkspur harbors a poison that is powerful enough to handle the pests, and the thought leaves one pleased that the pretty larkspur is good for something besides its beauty. The *D. consolida* is known as the forking larkspur and the *D. ajacis* as the rocket larkspur. Both are beauties of the field that one can scarcely overlook.

WOUNDS

Whether we speak of Indians or frontiersmen and their families, we are remembering people who lived close to nature. Hunting was a necessity. Fighting was not unusual. We do not wonder that it was necessary to find some ways of treating wounds.

The prickly pear, *Opuntia humifusa*, is in itself a healer. We may bind the peeled stems of the prickly pear over the cut as we would a bandage. Explorers looked upon it as an obstacle and a nuisance, but in the spring the blossom of the prickly pear is one of the beauties of the prairies, sunshiny yellow and splashy with color against the newly greened grasslands.

Maximilian spoke of the "snake root, perhaps *Aristolochia serpentaria*, which is said immediately to stanch the most violent bleeding of any wound."[4] Aristolochiaceae is the birthwort or wild ginger family, and *A. serpentaria* is commonly known as Virginia snakeroot. Naturally it was supposed to have snakebite antidotal properties, too, but apparently wounds could be treated by binding parts of the plant to the bleeding cut. He

[4]Maximilian, *Travels*, Vol. 1, p. 95.

found his snakeroot on the eastern coast near Delaware Gap,
and colonists knew it, not Indians. It is found west to Missouri.

The prairie ground-cherry, *Physalis lanceolata*, made a root
decoction for open wounds. One wonders if such a versatile
plant medicine was brewed and bottled for a primitive
medicine shelf such as we might have in our bathrooms today.
White settlers might have done so, but nomad Indians would
scarcely have carried such medicines with them as they moved
from summer homes to wintering quarters.

Brittle willow or crack willow, *Salix fragilis*, could be stripped
of its bark to make an astringent skin medicine to stop bleeding, or a poultice on sores. Some called it the tree-snap willow,
stag's head, redwood, or varnished willow. In fact, several
willows were valuable for skin healing. The leaves of the
prairie willow, *Salix humilis* (low willow, bush willow, dwarf
willow), could stop heavy bleeding when bound as a poultice.

Prickly pear
Opuntia polycantha

The bark of the shining or glossy willow, *S. lucida*, was said to be even better.

The dried bark of the flowering dogwood, *Cornus florida*, was esteemed in the South, where it grows well, for making a mild astringent liquid to stop bleeding. The eucalyptus tree, *Eucalyptus globulus*, was known on the West Coast; the dried leaves were made into a poultice or a wash to stop bleeding from wounds.

The berries of smooth sumac, *Rhus glabra*, were gathered for the same purpose. Other shrubs included the witch hazel, *Hamamelis virginiana*, the leaves of which were steeped for their healing properties. Its virtues are questioned by druggists, but that made no difference—witch hazel has long been popular as a lotion.

Various blackberries are said to have value in the dried bark of their rhizomes, including the *Rubus cuneifolius*, *R. nigrobaccus*, and *R. villosus*, though we cannot vouch for any of them personally.

Pipsissewa, *Chimaphila umbellata*, had its popularity as a liquid to heal cuts and bleeding, too. Pipsissewa is a pretty flower, but the dried leaves were the necessary ingredient.

Near streams and in swampy places you can find the odd stems of *Equisetum* species, one of which, the wood rush or sylvan horsetail, *E. sylvaticum*, was said to stop the flow of blood from wounds if it was pulverized as a poultice. Lacking that, the bark of the eastern hemlock tree, *Tsuga canadensis*, was as good to stop the bleeding.

Cook and pound bark of the white spruce, *Picea glauca*, to poultice wound cuts or swellings resulting from a wound. Some call it pine spruce, cat pine, cat spruce, single spruce, or skunk spruce. The high mountain spruce named Engelmann's spruce, *Picea engelmanni*, is said to be a variation of *P. glauca*, and could well be a substitute. In a like manner, the inner bark of the chokecherry, *Prunus virginiana*, must be pounded as a wound poultice, both healing and sedative.

The root of the curled dock, *Rumex crispus*, had an astringent quality that aided in healing cuts when pounded and placed on the cut as a poultice, or one could simmer the bark and leaves of the quaking aspen, *Populus tremuloides*, for cuts and wounds, sore arms or legs.

Flowering dogwood
Cornus florida

Smooth sumac
Rhus glabra

Curly dock
Rumex crispus

Needles of Engelmann's spruce
Picea engelmannii

A root wash brewed from the large-toothed aspen, *Populus grandidentata*, was made to stop excessive bleeding. Skunk cabbage, *Symplocarpus foetidus*, was treated in different ways. As a poultice, the root was dried, powdered, and sprayed over the surface of the wound. Root hairs alone were applied to stop excessive bleeding. The leaf bases were a poultice to reduce swellings. This plant of many names is an evil-smelling thing, but people in some sections still believe in the worth of the roots.

Roots of either edible valerian, *Valeriana edulis*, or bog valerian, *V. uliginosa*, were pounded to a pulp to poultice cuts and stop pain or bleeding.

Engelmann's spruce
Picea engelmannii

The prairie mushrooms sometimes called puffballs, *Lycoperdon* spp., were once a styptic for wounds. Dried, they were a talcum-powder dust to cure chafing on Indian babies. Even today our pharmacopoeias list *Lycoperdon* spores as a hemostatic or a surgical dusting powder.

Surgical and antiseptic healing dusting powder was made from several *Lycopodium* species, including the spores of shining clubmoss, *L. lucidulum*; the ground cedar, *L. complanatum*; and the ground pine, *L. obscurum*. The lycopodiums have several interesting popular names. Shining clubmoss is also called trailing evergreen or moonfruit pine; the ground cedar is called trailing Christmas green, festoon pine, crowfoot, ground pine, hogbed, or creeping jennie; and the real ground pine is called spiral pine, treelike clubmoss, or bunch evergreen.

Similarly, various lichens have been used. A handbook recently issued by the Smithsonian Institution reports that extracts of some lichens are powerful antibiotics, and in Finland a salve is made from lichens to treat burns and cuts.

Lady fern, *Athyrium filix-femina*, was made into a powdered dry root form and dusted over sores to heal them. Or one held matted cotton grass fuzz, *Eriophorum callithrix*, against the bleeding. Cotton grass was also called hare's-tail, sheathed cotton grass, cotton rush, cannadown, catlocks, and moss crops.

Lacking those plants, you could make a liquid from the five-flowered stiff gentian, *Gentiana quinquefolia*, which was another said to stop even hemorrhage. Raw sores reacted better to root of common horse gentian, *Triosteum perfoliatum*, pounded to a poultice and applied.

If a wound is infected you might try inserting a sliver of slippery elm inner bark into the wound. Slippery elm, *Ulmus rubra*, seems to have a healing quality that was as good in poultices, too.

It was said that swellings from wounds could be reduced by applying large flowered merrybells or bellwort, *Uvularia grandiflora*. Ostrich fern, *Pteretis pensylvanica*, was another leaf poultice. You will have to pound the root of the heart-leaved umbrellawort, *Mirabilis nyctaginea*, but you will have a poultice said to be especially good for sprains and swelling.

The root of the wood betony, *Pedicularis canadensis*, was

made into a poultice for external swellings. Such was the belief in its power that the whole plant, also called lousewort, was boiled for a tea drunk for internal swellings as well. Some folks went so far as to say the medicine would even cure tumors.

The pleurisy root or butterfly weed, *Asclepias tuberosa*, which flaunts its orange-yellow clustered flowers as the brightest of the milkweeds, offers its roots for two prescriptions. Chew the root to make a paste for wounds, or dry the root to make a pulverized powder which may be blown into a cut.

The inner bark of the speckled alder, *Alnus rugosa*, just as you find it is a poultice to reduce swelling. The bark is slightly astringent in its effect.

Burdock, *Arctium minus*, provided a root salve that reduced swelling on wounds as well as promoting healing on general skin infections.

The decoction made by digging the roots of the wild four-o'clock, *Mirabilis nyctaginea*, and the roots of the purple coneflower, *Echinacea angustifolia*, and boiling them together reduced swellings of arms or legs, but if one would treat an open wound directly he must chew the root of the prairie allionia or wild four-o'clock and blow the root bits into the wound.

The practice of chewing a part of a plant to make a poultice for a wound does not sound appetizing, but it was an accepted practice with other plants as well. The root of the hops, *Humulus lupulus*, "down three or four feet in the ground,"[5] was chewed and applied to wounds.

The scarlet globe mallow, *Sphaeralcea coccineum*, was prepared in this way, too, but we find that one chewed the plant, which would indicate leaves and stems, to apply to inflamed sores or wounds as a cooling salve. The scarlet globe mallow likes dry soil and can be found in abundance in plains lands.

Maximilian in his journey of 1832 and 1833 mentions that

a kind of bark which is now much used is that of the slippery elm [*Ulmus rubra*]: if chewed, or softened for a moment in water, it dissolves into a viscous slime, and is found very useful in dressing

[5]Melvin R. Gilmore, *Uses of Plants by the Indians of the Missouri River Region*. Bureau of American Ethnology report 1911–1912. Washington, D.C.: Government Printing Office, 1919, p. 77.

23

wounds, as it is cooling, and allays the inflammation. It is said to have
been applied with success in cholera, and is now sold, in powder, in
all the apothecaries' shops. A teaspoonful of this bark in boiling water
makes a very useful beverage, which is sweetened with sugar, and
has the same effect as linseed.[6]

Slippery elm or red elm is accurately referred to as *Ulmus
rubra* today, but its merits are still known. Chew the inner
bark, and it tastes good. The slippery substance is included in
some brands of cough drops as a soothing ingredient.

What was the "effect as linseed" mentioned by Maximilian?
Linseed is flaxseed, and flaxseed is in certain medicines today
as well.

Rippleseed plantain, *Plantago major*, and blackseed plantain,
P. rugelii, are known today as they were yesterday for their
value. There is nothing better to extract a thorn or splinter from
the flesh than the plantain, they say. Heat its leaves and apply.
For a swelling, turn the top of the leaf toward the skin. For
skin inflammations, ulcers, intermittent feverish skin, or bleeding, place the underside of the leaf on the skin. Ask any
old-timer, he will tell you that it is bound to work.

The leaves of the giant or great St.-John's-wort, *Hypericum
ascyron*, healed wounds by application, much as plantain
leaves.

In water ponds look for the yellow water lily or pond lily,
Nuphar advena. You need the underwater stems. Pull, dry, and
powder, then poultice over cuts, especially if the wounds have
begun to swell or are sore.

The evening primrose, *Oenothera biennis*, can be soaked as a
poultice. This is a rather pretty yellow flower; you can find its
blossom open in the early morning or late afternoon.

Three other roots were prepared by drying and pulverizing,
but not by chewing. The blue flag or iris, *Iris versicolor* and *I.
missouriensis*, can be beneficial for wounds. Pulverize the rootstock, make a paste, and apply.

Sweetroot roots are also pulverized to a paste. Sometimes
called sweet cicely, *Osmorhiza longistylis*, it is found in damp
wooded places such as one might see in foothill country or
along river breaks, but beware of its resemblance to poison or
water hemlock. If you are not sure of its identity, leave it alone.

[6]Maximilian, *Travels*, Vol. 1, p. 167.

Evening primrose
Oenothera biennis

Sweet cicely
Osmorhiza longistylis

Fireweed
Epilobium angustifolium

Sometimes a liquid decoction seems to soothe a throbbing wound better than a paste. Such an infusion can be made of the leaves of the yarrow or milfoil, *Achillea millefolium*. Steep the leaves as you would a tea, and bathe to lessen a swelling. This should stop the bleeding of the wound as well. It is said that in Scotland the yarrow leaves were mixed with a fat to make an ointment for a cut.

Wild indigo, *Baptisia leucantha*, was combined with other plants to make a medicine for ax or knife wounds, or for any kind of sores that resisted healing.

Swelling was also washed by a root decoction made from fireweed, *Epilobium angustifolium*, called the great willow herb, a brew having an astringent effect.

25

Bur oak
Quercus macrocarpa (photograph: Della B. Vik)

Western blue flag
Iris missouriensis

Yarrow
Achillea millefolium

Camomile tea was liked on frontiers to reduce fever and inflammation in wounds and slight sprains. For this we must pick the blossoms of the German camomile, *Matricaria chamomilla*, and dry them for later convenience. Only the flower heads are needed. This is an annual a little over a foot high with delicate lacy foliage and white daisy-shaped flowers.

We have not found many references to medications for broken bones, but one tree was remembered of value in bandaging a broken foot or leg. The bark of the bur oak, *Quercus macrocarpa*, was stripped as a bandage over the broken area.

In spite of its narcotic action, the farmers in North Carolina once used the jimsonweed, *Datura stramonium*, for wounds by applying the leaf on an infected portion. They also looked for comfrey, *Symphytum officinale*. The course comfrey plant is not

27

a beauty in spite of its purplish flowers, but its mucilaginous
root was crushed to a pulp for a poultice to place over the
infection. It has been known as healing herb, knitback, ass-ear,
backwort, blackwort, bruisewort, bum plant, and slippery root.

INTERNAL PARASITES

If it is necessary to use a vermifuge, try the same brew of roots
of wild four-o'clock, *Mirabilis nyctaginea*, and purple coneflower, *Echinacea angustifolia*, that was used to reduce swellings.
Drink the decoction as a proper medication.

Another recipe mixes the wood and inner bark of bur oak,
Quercus macrocarpa, with the sticky berries of staghorn sumac,
Rhus typhina, and the root of the flowering spurge, *Euphorbia
corollata*, a brew said to be especially effective against pinworms. The *Euphorbia* is a strong purge in itself.

A simpler remedy is that of the American filbert, *Corylus
americana*. Pick the nuts, but use only the prickles on the burs
of the husk to expel the worms. Whether you eat the prickles
raw or boil them, we do not know.

You can make a tea of the leaves of the leadplant, *Amorpha
canescens*, and drink it to kill pinworms. The leadplant in
blossom is a pretty plant, its lavender spikes easily seen on a
two- or three-foot high shrub.

The root of the swamp milkweed, *Asclepias incarnata*, was
boiled to make a tea drunk as a vermifuge with some effect.

The drug wormseed or goosefoot, *Chenopodium ambrosioides*
var. *anthelminticum*, is recognized today for its vermifuge properties. The wormseed goosefoot is also commonly called Mexican tea or American wormseed. It has a disagreeable odor, but
the volatile oil distilled from the ripe fruit or entire plant is
considered valuable enough for commercial cultivation in central Maryland.

Root tea made from the crested wood fern, *Dryopteris cristata*,
was regarded apprehensively by white settlers as a stomach
remedy, but taken as a drastic measure to kill intestinal worms.
Less drastic perhaps was tea made from the leaves of boneset,
Eupatorium perfoliatum, a tea drunk for various maladies besides
worms.

Staghorn sumac
Rhus typhina

The root of blue flag or iris, *Iris versicolor*, was eaten raw or drunk in a tea; and limber honeysuckle or the medaddy-bush, *Lonicera dioica*, could be effective when the berries and root bark were steeped together.

Bogbean or buckbean, *Menyanthes trifoliata*, would get rid of intestinal worms if you took a large enough dose of bogbean tea. It acts as a purge by inducing vomiting and evacuating the intestines all at the same time—a violent action that no worm could possibly withstand.

The root-bark tea made from red mulberry, *Morus rubra*, was supposed to be good for any sickness, so of course expelled worms from the system. Root tea from self-heal, *Prunella vulgaris*, was another worm killer.

29

Bracken
Pteridium aquilinum

Leadplant
Amorpha canescens

It is strange to contemplate, but the bracken or brake, *Pteridium aquilinum*, was considered soothing when the leaves were boiled in a syrup, but a root tea boiled into a strong decoction was anything but soothing for worms. It was said to be one of the better remedies.

The root bark of the American black currant, *Ribes americanum*, was steeped to make a remedy, and the leaves of eastern arborvitae, *Thuja occidentalis*, made another worm tea. A root tea perhaps not so widely known for tapeworms was that made from the edible valerian, *Valeriana edulis*.

Artemisia absinthium is known as wormwood, naturally because it was said to get rid of worms. One dried the leaves and the flowering tops. Mixed properly, this is either a mild tonic, a worm medicine, or that green alcoholic liquor called absinthe. It has been noted that continued use causes a nervous derangement, or to put it bluntly the stuff is narcotic if you take too much. But it gets rid of worms.

Another *Artemisia* is *A. puciflora*, no familiar name that we could find. This, too, was a worm repellent, not as commonly known as the other.

Pumpkin seeds raised in frontier gardens were a usual resort when wild plants were not within gathering distance. To control worms one should gather the ripe seeds of pumpkin, *Cucurbita pepo*, heat the kernels with water, add sugar to make them palatable, and drink. We hope it worked.

BURNS, ABRASIONS, RASHES, AND SKIN INFECTIONS

BURNS

There are two things that can be done about burns—either you prevent them or you soothe them after they occur. We do not know just why, but something in the components of two plants, scarlet globe mallow, *Sphaeralcea coccineum,* and the purple coneflower, *Echinacea angustifolia,* acted as a burn preventive. Both of these very versatile plants were invaluable to medicine men for impressing their clients.

To use the scarlet globe mallow as a burn preventive, the challenger of heat chewed the plant to a paste, then rubbed the paste over hands and arms, after which the treated hand could be dipped into a kettle of boiling water without ill effects. The flower has been called red false mallow or prairie mallow.

The purple coneflower was simpler. All the show-off had to do was to bathe his hands and arms with the raw juice of the plant, after which he could pick up anything hot and live to tell the tale. The purple coneflower was sometimes thrown into the steam bath, too; its anesthetic qualities made the resultant steam more endurable, hence the bather would absorb more heat and more value from his bath. The purple coneflower is a

Cattail
Typha latifolia

pretty blossom as wild blossoms go, and could well be a centerpiece on a table if one did not know that it had so many other virtues.

If you have been careless with fire, there is nothing to do but try to cool the burned flesh and wink back the tears. If you are lucky you might be seated beside a marsh where there is cattail, *Typha latifolia*, and you can pick one of the brown cattail cobs for its soothing down. Break it open and spread the down on the burn as you would antiseptic cotton. There! Feel better? Next time don't believe everything you hear about purple cone-flower keeping you from getting burned.

Other poultices for burned skin were made from the leaves or roots or even flowers of various plants. The simplest poul-

Purple coneflower
Echinacea angustifolia

Hound's-tongue
Cynoglossum officinale

Scarlet globemallow
Sphaeralcea coccineum

tices were just fresh leaves applied to the skin with no further treatment. Pick the leaves of the little candle anemone, *Anemone cylindrica*, sometimes called thimbleweed; or perhaps it would be easier to find the leaves of the Canada sagebrush, *Artemisia canadensis*, called Canada wormwood, sea wormwood, or wild wormwood. The tongue-shaped fresh leaves of the hound's-tongue, *Cynoglossum officinale*, sometimes called northern wild comfrey, were another.

36

Wild geranium
Geranium maculatum

Candle anemone
Anemone cylindrica

If you have rippleseed plantain, *Plantago major*, you can make a soothing burn wash effective for scalds from steeping the leaves.

Several roots were valued either as a poultice or a wash. Macerate the root of the heart-leaved umbrellawort, *Mirabilis nyctaginea*, for a burn poultice; or make a root poultice from the wild geranium or wild cranesbill, *Geranium maculatum*. Blood-root, *Sanguinaria canadensis*, was once thought to be a fine burn

Burdock
Arctium minus

Bloodroot
Sanguinaria canadensis

remedy. Root tea was made to bathe the burn, or one could chew the root to soften it and make a poultice.

Another root tea was steeped from the noble or showy goldenrod, *Solidago speciosa*, which was said to heal burns or a scalding from steam. An external salve was made from the root of the smaller burdock, *Arctium minus*, that seemed to help a burn. The root of the sweet flag or calamus root, *Acorus calamus*, was mixed with certain other unidentified plants for the same purpose.

There are various kinds of sunflowers, but for healing burns you must find the flowers of the sawtooth sunflower, *Helianthus grosseserratus*, and make a poultice.

39

Wild plum
Prunus americana

ABRASIONS

For just general skin care, try the soapweed, Spanish bayonet, or dagger plant, *Yucca glauca*, which was made into soap for washing hair or any part of the body. They dug the root for this, hence one of its names, the soapweed. *Yucca* is a spiky-leaved plant with tall shoots of whitish-green flowers, truly a startling sight in full bloom. It is found on dry hillsides over the plains. Once having found the *Yucca*, you can never forget it.

For skin abrasions, we must find a thicket of wild plum, *Prunus americana*, and dig a few roots. Scrape the bark of the roots, boil, and apply as a soothing wash.

40

Soapweed
Yucca glauca

Tansy
Tanacetum vulgare

Dry blossoms of the blue-berried elder, *Sambucus cerulea*, can be steeped for a skin lotion and antiseptic wash. The dried flowers of the American elder, *Sambucus canadensis*, were thought to have a healing power as a skin lotion even more than *S. cerulea*, and were used to treat sores, blisters, or even hemorrhoids.

The leaves of the tansy, *Tanacetum vulgare*, were soaked in buttermilk for nine days to make a skin lotion. The tansy leaves contain tanacetin oil, which is known to be toxic to man and

42

Northern bedstraw
Galium boreale

animals if eaten, but it is possible that it might not be dangerous as an external lotion.

The inner bark of the trunk or twigs of smooth sumac, *Rhus
glabra*, was steeped to make an astringent, but if you want a
poultice to concentrate on one spot the sumac leaves would be
better. It might be well to remind you that some people are
allergic to all *Rhus* species, and for them the sumac poultice
would not be advisable.

Witch hazel has been known for centuries as a lotion. Cut

43

Bearberry
Arctostaphylos uva-ursi

twigs from the shrub, *Hamamelis virginiana*, simmer, and add a small amount of alcohol if available. It is believed that oils in the shrub are of higher quality in late fall and winter.

The bark of the bur oak, *Quercus macrocarpa*, makes another good astringent; and agrimony, *Agrimonia gryposepala*, was once gathered by the settlers for the same reason. If you want an astringent with slightly styptic qualities, make a wash of the dried leaves and flowering tops of horseweed or fleabane, *Erigeron canadensis*. Look for the small panicled heads of greenish-white flowers.

The tannin content in prairie meadowsweet, *Filipendula rubra*, gave astringent properties known by many; and several *Galium* species were searched for skin diseases. Sometimes called wild baby's breath, the *Galium* species have their own names too. Shining bedstraw, *G. concinnum*, was valued as well as northern bedstraw, *G. boreale*, and small bedstraw, *G. trifidum*. Usually a plant tea was made as a wash, and the *Galium* solution was considered strong enough for eczema and ringworm besides the milder infections of the skin.

An antiseptic wash was made from the checkerberry or wintergreen, *Gaultheria procumbens*. A leaf extract of bearberry, *Arctostaphylos uva-ursi*, was an astringent; or boiled inner bark of the hackberry tree, *Celtis occidentalis*.

POISON RASHES

Living close to nature, the primitive Indians must have had every reason for finding a poison-ivy antidote. The pioneers could not always be on the alert for poison ivy or poison oak either, and nettles might snare one unaware that such nuisances were near. Let's be really honest. Even today, we who picnic in the woods or walk the prairies sometimes come home with poison rash. What to do about it? There were several remedies in the shrubs, flowers, little inconspicuous plants.

The smooth sumac, *Rhus glabra*, was one. This autumn brilliance is a touch of scarlet in the hills and is found in rolling hillocks over the plains as well. If you come home with your skin breaking in the itchy red rash of ivy poisoning, gather leaves of the smooth sumac and poultice the spot with the leaves. If this does not work, break some twigs of the red osier dogwood, *Cornus stolonifera*, from the banks of lakes or streams and boil the bark of the twigs until it makes a strong decoction. Wash the itchy skin again and again.

There is a small green plant with heart-shaped appendages called shepherd's purse, *Capsella bursa-pastoris*, so delicate in its stem and leaves that one must steep the whole plant, then wash the poisoned skin with the liquid. It was said to be a good cure not only for poison ivy but also for any sores on the skin.

If it still bothers, there are the jewelweeds, called snapweeds and touch-me-nots. The pale snapweed, *Impatiens pallida*, has pale yellow blossoms spurred and dainty along a slender stem. Crush the stems and leaves to a pulp and apply. The juice in the stems and leaves is the potent factor.

The spotted snapweed, *Impatiens capensis*, differs in the color of its flowers, orange with purple spots but spurred like its paler cousin. The jewelweeds are fine to soothe poison ivy, poison sumac, poison oak, or nettle—anything that dislikes the human skin. Incidentally, that name "touch-me-not" is not a warning to mankind for man's protection, but for its own. If you would like to try, the ripe pods explode when touched, scattering the seeds in all directions.

The touch-me-nots are good for eczema rashes, too, or if you use the fresh plant as a poultice the spotted snapweed will help any skin sore. A strange fact connecting the two snapweeds is that almost all of the popular names given one is for the other as well. They are called spotted touch-me-not, wild touch-me-not, silverleaf, balsam, jewelweed, speckled jewels, silverweed, slipperweed, earjewel, pocket drop, eardrop, wild celandine, brook celandine, solentine, shining grass, weathercock, kicking-colt, kicking-horses, and wild balsam.

A fluid is extracted from the sticky-heads or gumweed, *Grindelia squarrosa*, which is messy but effective when combined with sugar of lead for poison-ivy treatment. An easier remedy is that of the Canada or wild lettuce, *Lactuca canadensis*. Rub the milky juice of the fresh plant directly on the rash. It has several popular names—tall lettuce, wild opium, trumpet milkweed, trumpets, trumpet weed, fireweed, butterweed, horseweed, devil's ironweed, and devil's-weed.

Red osier dogwood
Cornus stolonifera

Shepherd's purse
Capsella bursa-pastoris

Curlycup gumweed
Grindelia squarrosa

The Virginia pepperweed, *Lepidium virginicum*, attacked poison ivy in two ways. Heat the plant in water and wash the poisoned area with the solution or poultice with the freshly bruised leaves. North Carolinians believed that sweet fern, *Comptonia peregrina*, made a tea as a poison-ivy antidote which should be drunk and bathed in as a double precaution.

If you have been stung by a nettle, *Urtica* spp., you can cure it by rubbing the nettle's own root on the sting. We tried it, and there may be some truth to the old belief. Although the sting remained for a short time it faded very rapidly, whereas without the root treatment the nettle's sting had us ruefully regarding our fingers for half a day.

48

ECZEMAS

If you are victimized by a mild itching, try washing the skin with a decoction made from the fruit of bush honeysuckle, *Diervilla lonicera*. A root infusion made from dotted gayfeather, *Liatris punctata*, was applied locally to cure an itch if you did not know what caused it. The Illinois bundleflower, spider bean, or prairie mimosa, *Desmanthus illinoensis*, was another cure for any itch. Here again we must boil the leaves to a strong decoction and wash the affected parts. Look for the greenish-white petals of this tall weed on the wet sandy soils. While you are near water, pick a few cattails if they are in season. The brown cattails last for months if kept in a dry place in the house, and the down is one of the most soothing things known to man for chafing as well as the burns and scalds we mentioned earlier. The cattail, *Typha latifolia*, is rather well scattered through the country.

The lady fern, *Athyrium filix-femina*, was gathered, its dry root powdered and dusted over sores. Boiled bark of the speckled alder, *Alnus rugosa*, made a good astringent, but if you dry the same bark and powder it fine you have another good powder for the relief of chafing.

Steeped leaves of the leadplant, *Amorpha canescens*, treated eczema as a wash; but the wild indigo plant, *Baptisia leucantha*, was combined with others to become effective against eczema. The boiled root of the wild indigo alone was good for sores.

If you boil fruits of the meadow rose, *Rosa blanda*, to a syrup, you have a medicine against any itch on the body.

An infusion made from the bark of the white ash, *Fraxinus americana*, was fine for sores or a skin itch, or one could make a salve by cooking the inner bark of the tree. The infusion has an astringent action, and was noted particularly for treating an itching scalp. Bark of red ash, *F. pennsylvanica*, can be steeped to make an astringent, too. One recognizes the red ash by the red hairs on the twigs and under leaves, the red-brown velvet of the buds, and the red inner bark.

Another cure for itchy skin was a liquid boiled from the roots of palmate-leaf sweet coltsfoot, *Petasites palmata*. The leaves of downy phlox, *Phlox pilosa*, were steeped for an eczema wash of some value; and another for skin eruptions is horsemint or

Dotted gayfeather
Liatris punctata

49

Wild rose hips
Rosa sp.

wild bergamot, *Monarda fistulosa*, its leaves boiled for a wash.

Eczema or rash was also said to be cured by application of fresh leaves of the yarrow, *Achillea millefolium*. The root of burdock, *Arctium minus*, when steeped and drunk was believed to be effective in combatting chronic skin diseases such as syphilis, or externally as a salve for skin eruptions and other skin irritations.

50

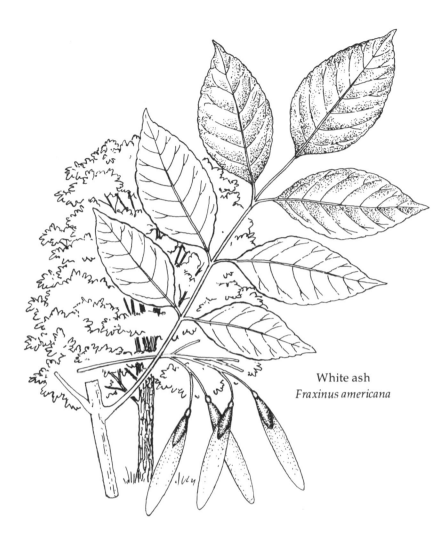

White ash
Fraxinus americana

The roots of leatherwood, or moosewood, *Dirca palustris*, were steeped to make a wash for chronic diseases, or the bark of the plant combined with sarsaparilla to make an external ointment for really bad skin diseases, even an ulcerated skin. Eczema and ulcers are also said to respond to a wash made from the root of narrow-leaved purple coneflower, *Echinacea angustifolia*.

51

Horsemint or wild bergamot
Monarda fistulosa (photograph: Marjorie Morcom)

Ringworm infection on the skin was a hazard in the early
days as it can be today, but one plant was considered strong
enough to cure it. For ringworm dig a jack-in-the-pulpit,
Arisaema triphyllum. Mix the juice of the fresh corm in lard to
make a salve for applying over the infection.

Eczema and other skin affections sometimes reacted well to
an oil obtained from birch, *Betula alba*, by distilling the bark
and wood, then adding steam to make an ointment that would
stay on the skin.

All skin diseases were assumed to be remedied by dried

Cow parsnip
Heracleum lanatum

violet plants. Canada violet, *Viola canadensis*, and American
dog violet, *V. conspersa*, were especially respected.

BOILS

Few things are as painful and unsightly as a boil. We suppose
that the remedy against its infection varied according to the
type of country in which one found oneself.

The cow parsnip, *Heracleum lanatum*, growing in wet woods

over the plains states, was handy at such a time. This big awkward plant is easy to see because it towers over so many of its neighbors, growing easily four feet high. One might think the broad sprawly leaves would be important, being such prominent parts of the plant's anatomy, but if we would treat a boil we must dig the root. The cow parsnip is also known as beaverroot, but we have not discovered the reason for that name. Nevertheless, dig the root, scrape or pound it fine, and simmer. With the scrapings of the boiled mixture, make a poultice and bind it on the painful boil. The fresh root pounded as a poultice is better for ordinary sores, and if you mix cow parsnip leaves with the root you have a mixture that will cause skin blisters as a counterirritant wherever needed. Cow parsnip root poultice was said to be effective against the feverish skin inflammation of erysipelas.

The roots of the sweet cicely, *Osmorhiza longistylis*, can be pounded for a poultice for a boil if cow parsnip is not handy. This member of the carrot family is found in damp wooded places in low foothills or open woods with its small white flower clusters a graceful note of beauty, but be very sure that you know it well. It strongly resembles the poison hemlock, *Conium maculatum*, and a mistake can be fatal.

The root of the American spikenard, *Aralia racemosa*, treated blood poisoning and was used as a poultice on infected sores. The plant has been known popularly as Indian spikenard, spignet, spiceberry, Indian root, petty morrel, life-of-man, and old-man's-root.

Wild sarsaparilla, *Aralia nudicaulis*, is also known as small spikenard among its popular names, and was a poultice, its root pounded and applied.

If none of these heal the boil, then try the pounded root of the Virginia anemone, *Anemone virginiana*, as a poultice, or the pounded root of fireweed, *Epilobium angustifolia*. The Virginia anemone can be called windflower, wood flower, nimble weed, or even wild cucumber. The fireweed has picked up a bunch of names. Call it great willow herb, spiked willow herb, bay willow, Persian willow, firetop, burntweed, French willow herb, bay willow herb, Indian wickup, herb wickopy, flowering willow, blooming sally, or sally-bloom.

If we don't want to take time to dig roots and pound them or stew them, we can always pick the green leaves of *Rumex crispus*, called yellow or curled dock or more loosely just sorrel. Crush the green leaves and bind on the boil as an immediate poultice. We do not know what will happen, but old-timers say it was once done.

You can make a poultice of the entire plant from hawk's-beard, *Crepis runcinata*, and have a medicine powerful enough to open a carbuncle or (it was said) even cancer so it could be excised without fear of complications. The hawk's-beard strongly resembles the common dandelion in its blossoms, but when you look closely you will see that the hawk's-beard's leaves are smooth and entire to toothed or jagged, somewhat like the leaves of the other plant but not quite. This is also called naked-stemmed hawk's-beard.

Once long ago, the root of poison ivy, *Rhus radicans*, was a rather dangerous medicine, pounded as a poultice to put on a swelling to make it open. One would think that it might have been contemplated only as a last resort.

The scarlet globe mallow, *Sphaeralcea coccineum*, was more a soothing salve. The gray leaves of the plant, also called red false mallow, have star-shaped hairs, and the poppy-colored blossom is striking above its muted stem. Parts of the plant were chewed to make a sort of paste, and its mucilaginous qualities acted as a cooling agent. At least it felt better than it had, and in a boil even that is something.

About the easiest remedy was pitch from the white pine, *Pinus strobus*. Smear the pitch over the boil and wait for its chemistry to "bring out the poison."[1] The inner bark of the white pine tree was pounded as a poultice for any kind of inflamed wound, sore, or ulcer, or if white pine was not available the Norway pine, *P. resinosa*, could be a substitute.

Boil the inner bark of American linden, *Tilia americana*, to make a poultice which will cause boils to open. Poultice made from the inner bark of slippery elm, *Ulmus rubra*, is about as good a remedy for infections as you can find for boils, abscesses, inflammations, sores, or infected wounds. Another root poultice was made from edible valerian, *Valeriana edulis*.

The quaking aspen, *Populus tremuloides*, has various proper-

[1] J. Almus Russell, "Doctoring with Herb's," *Frontiers*, February 1957. Academy of Natural Sciences of Philadelphia, 1957. p. 81.

ties for skin troubles. The buds can be boiled to make an antiseptic liquid. The bark and leaves steeped together make an external wash for gangrenous wounds, eczema, burns, body odor, or even cancer, though it is highly questionable whether the liquid application on the skin ever helped the cancer much. The same concoction was said to reduce arterial swellings when taken as an internal medicine.

Sluggish ulcers and sores were treated by a salve made from the dried winter leafbuds collected in the spring from the southern poplar, *Populus deltoides* var. *missouriensis*, the balm of Gilead buds, *X Populus gileadensis*, or the similar balm of Gilead, *Populus nigra*. The sticky buds were boiled in fat to make the salve, which was also found to be antiseptic in treating wounds. A skin lotion was made from these *Populus* species by covering the buds with alcohol for two days.

Infected sores sometimes reacted to a root poultice from the starry silene, called starry campion or Thermon snakeroot, *Silene stellata*.

For sores of long standing, a poultice was made from the pounded root or the leaves of the thin-leaved sunflower, *Helianthus decapetalus*, also called wild sunflower; or perhaps a poultice of the leaves of St. Louis sagebrush, *Artemisia ludoviciana*, dark-leaved mugwort, or western mugwort.

Boil root of glade mallow, *Napaea dioica*, and you have a poultice that will not only soften old sores but will lessen swellings that may have developed.

The leaves of the American alumroot, *Heuchera americana*, had an astringent quality for healing sores; and bark of common winterberry, *Ilex verticillata*, was astringent enough to tackle ulcers and skin eruptions.

For really deep-seated inflammations you would need the eastern larch or tamarack, *Larix laricina*. Get some bark from the trunk or root. Make a poultice of the fresh bark to place over the inflamed area. Steep the rest of the bark to make a tea, which taken internally was believed to drive out the inflammation from within the body, at the same time generating heat over the entire body.

The leaves of eastern arborvitae, *Thuja occidentalis*, made an external ointment supposed to cure ulcers, warts, and cancerous growths.

MISCELLANEOUS SKIN PROBLEMS

Heat rash reacted favorably to a poultice made from the leaves of the slim nettle, *Urtica gracilis*, soaked in warm water and applied.

The intense skin inflammation of erysipelas was treated by a root concoction of big merrybells, *Uvularia grandiflora*.

Skin inflammations accompanied by fever were treated by a root tea from black sanicle, *Sanicula marilandica*, as often called black snakeroot.

If you have the yellow skin of jaundice, you could drink tea from butter-and-eggs, *Linaria vulgaris*, to attack the condition from within. The tea was believed to be of benefit for skin eruptions too. The fresh flowers were added to a skin ointment for hemorrhoidal tumors and skin diseases, though the skin tumors were also treated by a poultice of the entire fresh plant.

Butter-and-eggs
Linaria vulgaris

Wild columbine
Aquilegia canadensis

American plane tree
Platanus occidentalis

Chronic jaundice was sometimes treated by drinking root extract of dandelion, *Taraxacum officinale*.

Smallpox scabs were washed with a bark infusion from the American plane tree, *Platanus occidentalis*. It was said to dry the sores and lessen the chance of scars.

If it becomes necessary to increase perspiration on the skin, the dried bark of the root of silky sassafras, *Sassafras albidum* var. *molle*, has been known for centuries as an agent. Similar effects have been attributed to the roots of wild columbine, *Aquilegia canadensis*; wild sarsaparilla, *Aralia nudicaulis*; burdock, *Arctium minus*; Atlantic yam, *Dioscorea villosa*; purple coneflower, *Echinacea angustifolia*; annual or daisy fleabane, *Erigeron annuus*; the dried leaves and flowering tops of the horseweed or fleabane, *Erigeron canadensis*, or the Philadelphia fleabane, *Erigeron philadelphicus*; the leaves and flowering tops of boneset, *Eupatorium perfoliatum*, as evidenced by one of its familiar names, the sweating plant; the dye bedstraw or small

59

Oriental cocklebur
Xanthium orientale

Dandelion
Taraxacum officinale

Philadelphia fleabane
Erigeron philadelphicus

cleavers, *Galium tinctorium*; or the lavender blossoms and leaves of *Monarda fistulosa*, called wild bergamot or horsemint. Both groundsels were valued, the golden groundsel, *Senecio aureus*, and the lamb's-tongue groundsel, *Senecio integerrimus*. Root tea from cup rosinweed, *Silphium perfoliatum*, could make you perspire as well as any of them, and flowering tops of blue verbena, *Verbena hastata*, were as effective.

If none of these are available in your vicinity, perhaps you can find the whole plant of the Oriental cocklebur, *Xanthium orientale*, to make you sweat, or steep a tea of prickly ash, *Zanthoxylum americanum*.

Surely one of these many plants can be found in your county someplace.

61

DISORDERS OF HEAD
AND THROAT

EARACHE

*D*id you ever have a sick child crying from earache? Poor little fellow. There isn't anything we wouldn't do for him if we could only make him feel better. If we lived on the wide lonely prairies in homestead days we would have tried the plant remedies without a qualm just on the bare chance that they might help.

Yarrow, *Achillea millefolium*, was probably the most common remedy, simply because it was the easiest to find. It grows almost anywhere, easy to identify with its lacy leaves and white small-blossomed heads. Our worried mothers wadded yarrow leaves moistened with an infusion made of boiling a small amount of yarrow leaves with water, and placed the wad in the ear.

Blue flag, *Iris versicolor*, has a rootstock valuable for earache. Pulverize the rootstock, mix with water, and drop in the ear. This pretty blue iris is also referred to as the fleur-de-lis among other names.

The root of the Canada wild ginger, *Asarum canadense*, was cooked and then used to poultice the ear.

American licorice, *Glycyrrhiza lepidota*, has a soothing quality that is recognized today. For earache one steeped the leaves for

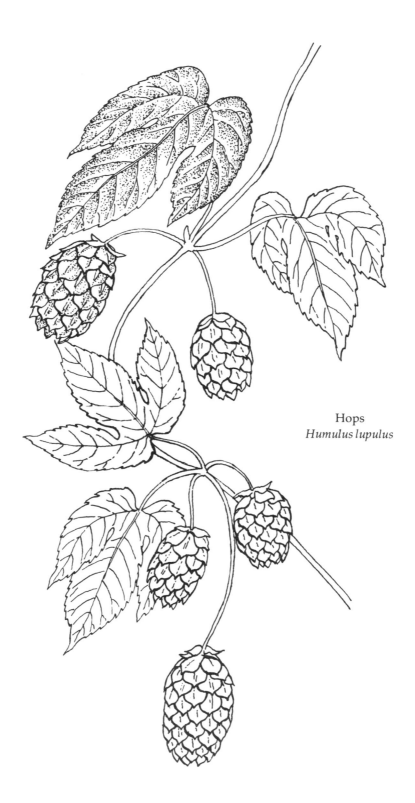

Hops
Humulus lupulus

63

Wild licorice
Glycyrrhiza lepidota

medicinal ear drops. They may not have cured, but they could
have lessened the pain.

Dried hops, *Humulus lupulus*, held in a bag against the ear
were good, or flaxseed, *Linum lewisii*, was helpful in the same
way. Here's another — mix some ground chestnuts with mutton tallow and poultice the ear.

If you know where you can find the mayweed or camomile,
Anthemis cotula, make a hot fomentation of the flowers with
water and vinegar for an ear wash when it aches.

64

Lewis flax
Linum lewisii

Ash trees, *Fraxinus* spp., were popular for a lot of reasons, one of them being an ear remedy. You need an ash stick, one end of which you stick into the campfire. As it slowly heats, the sap from the stick is supposed to bubble from it. Catch the warmed sap as it appears, because that warmed sap is what one must put in an aching ear to relieve the pain. Perhaps it was the temperature of the sap, or perhaps there was some ingredient in it that helped. We do not know, but it seems to have worked for earaches of the past.

In those days when no eye doctors were available for hundreds
of miles of frontier country, when the primitive Indians had no
thought of such help whatsoever, the blue flag, *Iris versicolor*,
was one of the flowers that gave its root for sore eyes as well as
earaches. The same mixture of pulverized rootstock, mixed
with water, could be dropped in the eyes if one had reached
that ultimate point where something must be done.

Sore eyes. What did they mean by the phrase? Infections?
Whatever caused the sore eyes, they had recourses other than
iris.

The Canada anemone, *Anemone canadensis*, called round-
leaved anemone or meadow anemone, was valued more for its
root than its fragile white flower. Boil the root and drop a little
liquid in the eyes. Good for cross-eye, twitching of the eyes,
even for cataract, they said.

If you have *Anemone cylindrica*, candle anemone or thimbleweed, steep the stem and fruit to make a wash for sore eyes.
White people used any of the anemones for the same purpose.

The rush skeleton plant or skeleton weed, *Lygodesmia juncea*,
also called rushlike lygodesmia, was boiled for sore-eye
medicine, but the stems were needed. This flower is called the
prairie pink or milk pink. It needs little persuasion to grow and
can be found on quite dry banks and plains country.

The bark of the black oak, *Quercus velutina*, was crushed and
boiled to make an infusion which was said to cure sore eyes.
Red maple, *Acer rubrum*, provided another bark infusion for
eyewash. The red maple is sometimes confused in its popular
names by being called hard, soft, scarlet, water, white, or
shoe-peg maple.

The root bark of American elm, *Ulmus americana*, was boiled
to make an eye lotion. The tree is known as white elm, water
elm, or swamp elm, a vivid tree often planted in lawns for
shade.

The inner bark of the little eastern wahoo, *Euonymus
atropurpurea*, was steeped to make an eyewash by some Indian
tribes, while others preferred the root bark of the tree.

Two plants recommended for weak or inflamed eyes were
the wild rose and the wolfberry. The wild rose is best in the

American elm
Ulmus americana

Leaves of American elm
Ulmus americana

Rosa arkansana var. *suffulta*, and one must steep the fruits to make the eyewash. Other names for the wolfberry, *Symphoricarpos occidentalis*, are buckbrush and snowberry. For eyewash the leaves were steeped, then the liquid was cooled to body temperature. The little white berries of the wolfberry are seen in dry thickets and hillsides.

In days when life depended on survival of the strongest, and one had to kill or be killed, it is said that the powder of the dried gem puffball, *Lycoperdon pyriforme*, was thrown in an enemy's eyes to blind him, causing permanent blindness. Nobody remembers it actually being done, but it is well to guard against an accidental occurrence.

Western snowberry
Symphoricarpos occidentalis

An eye remedy, though not necessarily for the puffball attack, was made from the sweet cicely, *Osmorhiza longistylis*. Another was the liquid balsam direct from the bark blister of the balsam fir, *Abies balsamea*.

If your eyes or mouth get twisted or crossed, you must find the sharp-lobed hepatica or liverleaf, *Hepatica acutiloba*. Make a root tea of the plant, wash the face with the tea daily, and take two teaspoons dosage daily until the face and eyes return to normal. We do not know whether it was effective or not.

For eyes that are sore, not crossed, steep blossoms of the smooth sumac, *Rhus glabra*, for an eyewash of curative properties. Several raspberries were sought to make an eyewash, the

69

Frost grape
Vitis vulpina

root being simmered to the desired strength. The western red raspberry, *Rubus idaeus aculeatissimus*, was one; the mountain blackberry, *Rubus allegheniensis*, and the dwarf red raspberry sometimes called eyeberry, *Rubus pubescens*, were others. The Allegheny blackberry root was also pounded and steeped for a poultice over the eye.

To reduce swelling of the eye a poultice was made of grated root of the snow trillium, *Trillium grandiflorum*, called large-flowered wake-robin, large-flowered trillium, white lilies, bath flower, or trinity lily, and held on the swollen eye.

The widely spread ragweed, *Ambrosia elatior*, was an eye remedy. Soak bandages in a leaf tea and lay them on sore eyes for relief.

The root of jack-in-the-pulpit, *Arisaema triphyllum*, was pounded and placed as a poultice over sore eyes, but it must be watched carefully. One is somewhat skeptical about the safety of these measures when dealing with anything as delicate as eyes, but they are part of American folklore and as that we report them.

Wild grapes, particularly the frost grape, *Vitis vulpina*, were prepared in two ways. Grape seeds removed foreign matter from the eye if a single irritation was bothering. If the job was bigger, the grape itself was crushed and the fresh juice washed "wild rice hulls from the eyes of the threshers or winnowers."[1]

Mountain maple, *Acer spicatum*, was best when one wanted to remove a particle from an eye. Find the pith of a twig for the job, and afterward make an eye lotion from soaked pith. *spicatum* has been called moose maple, swamp maple, water maple, and low maple.

HEADACHE

When we get to the subject of headaches we might as well admit immediately that the purple coneflower, *Echinacea angustifolia*, was a headache cure, too. They burned the tops and inhaled the smoke. It probably did the job, too, but if for

[1]Huron H. Smith, *Ethnobotany of the Menomini Indians.* Bulletin of the Public Museum of the City of Milwaukee, Vol. 4, No. 1. Milwaukee, Wisconsin: December 10, 1923. P. 58.

Western red raspberry
Rubus idaeus aculeatissimus

Hemp dogbane
Apocynum cannabinum

Spreading dogbane
Apocynum androsaemifolium

some reason it did not, our forebears had other flowers which they could try.

They inhaled smoke from the burning root of the Indian hemp, *Apocynum cannabinum*, and the spreading dogbane, *A. androsaemifolium*; or the whole plant of hound's-tongue, *Cynoglossum* spp.

The scent of the daisy fleabane, *Erigeron ramosus*, called sweet scabious, was inhaled by some for treating a sick headache, though it was much too simple a remedy for others.

While the coals are burning, toss some dried leaves of bracken, *Pteridium aquilinum*, on them to smoke, too. They may have some effect.

The most direct in its application was the jack-in-the-pulpit, *Arisaema triphyllum*, that quaint greenish elf of the Midwestern woodlands in his striped pulpit. Dry the corm, pulverize well, rub the resultant dust directly on the top of head or the temples, wherever the ache is most persistent.

A gentler treatment is that made with the big-leaved aster, *Aster macrophyllus*; one bathes the head with a root-tea solution to obtain relief.

A poultice to be applied directly to the head may be made from the pulverized root of the wild cucumber, *Echinocystis lobata*, as often called the balsam apple.

If you have spotted snapweed, *Impatiens capensis*, crush the plant to obtain the fresh juice and rub the juice on your aching forehead.

To attack the headache indirectly, we can make several kinds of tea that may be drunk as an antidote. Gather the tiny black seeds of the wild columbine, *Aquilegia canadensis*, crush in hot water, and drink. Look down into the seed pods of the columbine from their raised open ends if you would catch a wild columbine with its black seeds still on the plant. They scatter quickly.

The root of the prairie ground-cherry, *Physalis lanceolata*, can hardly get away from us. Gather this plant from the prairies in the west and boil the root. We would advise taking the dosage in very small quantities at first if you must live dangerously. Who knows how strong it may be?

The Virginia ground-cherry, *Physalis virginiana*, was boiled, leaves, stems, root, and all, to make a tea for dizziness. A

Golden alexanders
Zizea aurea

Canada mayflower
Maianthemum canadense

headache with dizzy spells was also treated by drinking a root tea made from the candle anemone, *Anemone cylindrica*. Leaves of eastern arborvitae, *Thuja occidentalis*, made a tea good for various other disorders as well.

A headache snuff was made by mixing the flower stalks of golden zizia, *Zizia aurea*, with the leaves of spotted bee balm, *Monarda punctata*, and the disk florets of Philadelphia fleabane, *Erigeron philadelphicus*. Oswego tea made from bee balm, *Monarda didyma*, was also said to help, or you can dry spotted bee balm leaves and flowers.

Mix the root of the false Solomon's seal, *Smilacina racemosa*,

74

White baneberry
Actaea pachypoda

and the spreading dogbane, *Apocynum androsaemifolium*, for a headache, too. If your headache is due to eyestrain, try a root tea made from the red baneberry, *Actaea rubra*, or the white baneberry, *Actaea pachypoda*, as was once done, though today's botanists warn you not to do so because the *Actaea* roots are a strong purgative.

The seeds of the cow parsnip, *Heracleum lanatum*, were gathered for another headache cure. *Maianthemum canadense*, bead-ruby or Canada mayflower, is so small that one must throw the whole plant in the kettle to make a headache tea.

75

Certain mouthwashes were of so gentle a nature that they were saved for babies, and will be discussed in the children's chapter. For the whole family, make a mouthwash by boiling root of spotted cranesbill, *Geranium maculatum*, a brew thought to help sore gums, pyorrhea, even neuralgia and toothache. This is also known as wild geranium.

Mouth sores could be treated by a root tea from bigroot lady's thumb, *Polygonum coccineum*; but if one hemorrhages from the mouth he must drink the bitter tea made from Pennsylvania smartweed, *Polygonum pennsylvanica*, called Pennsylvania persicaria too.

Canker in the mouth could react to a bark tea solution from the American plum tree, *Prunus americana*; some thought an ulcerated mouth should be better treated by a root concoction from large-flowered merrybells, *Uvularia grandiflora*.

On the other hand, if what you need is something to promote the flow of saliva in the mouth, you might try the bark of the toothache tree, *Zanthoxylum clavaherculis*, correctly called the prickly ash. If that is not handy, find root of narrow-leaved purple coneflower, *Echinacea angustifolia*, and chew the root for its juice. Others considered acceptable were the mouthwashes steeped from root of blue flag, *Iris versicolor*; the oriental cocklebur, *Xanthium orientale*; tea from another prickly ash, *Zanthoxylum americanum*; or root of skunk cabbage, *Symplocarpus foetidus*.

Say you have a sore throat but you don't know why—try a tea from the purple flower spikes of the self-heal or heal-all, *Prunella vulgaris*. Your throat is inflamed? Simmer the berries of smooth sumac, *Rhus glabra*, for a gargle. If you should swallow some of the mixture, don't worry. It tastes so much like lemonade that some folks made it just as a pleasant beverage.

Root tea from black sanicle (black snakeroot), *Sanicula marilandica*, may not taste as good but it probably was as effective for a sore throat, particularly when a fever was involved. For a swollen throat, boil the flowers of the stiff goldenrod, *Solidago rigida*, called hard-leaved goldenrod. A mild gargle was made from the root of Canada wild ginger, *Asarum canadense*; or from the seeds of the wild senna, *Cassia*

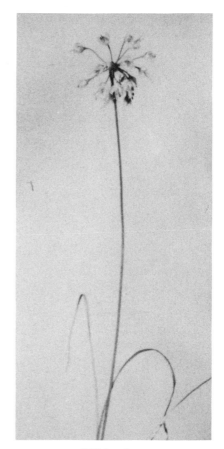

Stiff goldenrod
Solidago rigida

Wild onion
Allium sp.
(photograph: Marjorie Morcom)

marylandica, soaked in water. Another throat gargle was that from the little Canada mayflower, *Maianthemum canadense*, a plant perhaps not so well known for its throat-healing properties as the horehound, *Marrubium vulgare*. For many centuries the horehound has been included in medicines for throat or lungs.

Laryngitis or spasmodic croup could be lessened by drinking a root decoction made of Seneca snakeroot, *Polygala senega*. Sometimes called mountain flax, it was a medicine to loosen the mucus in the throat. An expectorant was also made from wild yam or Atlantic yam root, *Dioscorea villosa*; and teas were made from daisy fleabane, *Erigeron annuus*, that white blossom

77

Red clover
Trifolium pratense

with a purple tinge; the whiter blossoms of the white top
fleabane, *Erigeron ramosus*; the leaves of the fragrant cudweed,
Gnaphalium obtusifolium; or bog valerian, *Valeriana uliginosa*.

The dried blossoms of red clover, *Trifolium pratense*, were
probably the easiest to find for a mucus-clearing medicine,
though wild onion was better known. The wild onion, *Allium*
spp., was sliced into a pan, sugar was laced liberally through it
to dissolve in the onion juice, and our grandmothers had
instant throat syrup.

The lavender pasqueflower, *Anemone patens*, found blooming
so early in the spring, was sometimes dried and the entire herb
simmered for a mucus expectorant, but it was dangerous. It

Pasqueflower
Anemone patens (photograph: Della B. Vik)

could cause vomiting, pain, tremors, and even a collapse of the patient if not handled properly. The root of purple-stem angelica, *Angelica atropurpurea*, was doubtless much safer. *Euphorbia pilulifera*, the pill-bearing spurge, was even listed in some of the pharmacy handbooks as an expectorant.

Maybe less known than these was the elecampane inula, *Inula helenium*, the dried rhizome of which was found to loosen mucus. In some areas bethroot or birthroot, *Trillium erectum*, could be located as a stimulating expectorant, its dark dull-purple petals a beauty of the woods that really should not be disturbed.

One could turn to the trees if the smaller plants were hard to

79

Pearly everlasting
Anaphalis margaritacea

Pussytoes
Antennaria plantaginifolia

find. The dried inner bark of white pine, *Pinus strobus*, would have the same effect. Early in the spring it was believed that one should collect the closed winter leaf buds of the *Populus nigra*, another tree known as the balm of Gilead, or the southern poplar, *Populus deltoides missouriensis*. Dry the leaf buds in the air to make them ready for use as an expectorant.

If the soreness extends to the tonsils you could make a throat gargle said to sooth chronic inflammation in that area from the inner bark of white oak, *Quercus alba*, or the bur oak, *Q.*

macrocarpa. A tea was also made from leaves of St. Louis sagebrush, *Artemisia ludoviciana,* particularly good for tonsillitis and sore throat.

Root tea from sweet cicely, *Osmorhiza longistylis,* was good for a sore throat, as was a brew made by mixing the root of false Solomon's seal, *Smilacina racemosa,* with rosy or spreading dogbane, *Apocynum androsaemifolium.* One could use the dog-banes alone to make root tea for throat trouble, either the *A. androsaemifolium* or the *A. cannabinum.*

The leaves and bark of the speckled or hoary alder, *Alnus rugosa,* were boiled to counteract inflammations of the mouth and throat. The dainty white flowers of pearly everlasting, *Anaphalis margaritacea,* were gathered by white settlers as a soothing throat syrup, as were those of a similar plant, the plantain-leaved pussytoes or plantain-leaved everlasting, *Antennaria plantaginifolia.*

NOSE

We hardly know where to place the plants that deal with the ancient bane of nosebleed, under a heading of "nose" or "headache."

Like the old-fashioned remedy of bleeding for a myriad of illnesses, once it was believed that a severe headache could be lessened by causing the nose to bleed. That was the purpose for which the prairie-dog weed, fetid marigold, false dog fennel, or prairie dog food, *Dyssodia papposa,* was gathered. We are not told how it caused nose bleeding, but besides the fact that the flower smelled horribly that was the only known reason for its growing. Its yellow blossoms are not open enough for beauty.

Fortunately our frontiersmen and their Indian friends had a remedy in case the nosebleed got out of hand. The white sagebrush, *Artemisia gnaphalodes,* which grows more or less plentifully on the driest prairies, could stop it. Place a pellet of chewed sage leaves in the nostril and worry no more. The leaves of the yarrow, *Achillea millefolium,* had a styptic quality to stop nosebleed, too, a fact that gave the name "nosebleed" to the plant as one of its popular names.

Blue-eyed grass
Sisyrinchium sp.

White sagebrush
Artemisia gnaphalodes

The root of the agrimony, *Agrimonia gryposepala*, was another to stop a persistent nosebleed if yarrow was not around, though we have found yarrow much easier to locate than the agrimony. Some call it tall, hairy agrimony, stickweed, or stickseed. The roots of the little-leaved buttercup, abortive crowfoot, kidney crowfoot, or smooth-leaved crowfoot, *Ranunculus abortivus*, would also work.

The clustered snakeroot, *Sanicula gregaria*, was burned on hot stones while one suffering from nosebleed stood close enough to inhale the fumes or steam from the plant.

Hay fever is neither a cold nor a fever, but does center its miseries most often in the nose. Blue-eyed grass, *Sisyrinchium* spp., was boiled to make a tea thought to cure hay fever.

83

The purple coneflower, *Echinacea angustifolia* or other *Echinacea* species, was the handiest flower to have around the back yard of any you might know. It was good for toothache, too.

The sweet flag or calamus root, *Acorus calamus*, had a sedative quality in its rootstock that could ease the jumping pain of a toothache. Chew the rootstock raw. If calamus root is not convenient you can chew the root of the wild licorice, *Glycyrrhiza lepidota*, too, and then hold it in the mouth.

Farther south around Arkansas and Texas a prickly ash grows that was more familiarly known as the toothache tree, *Zanthoxylum clavaherculis*. The bumpy bark is hot to taste and will help a toothache. So deeply entrenched in the affections of the people has this weird tree become that it has accumulated several other names including the sting tongue, the tear blanket, wait-a-bit, southern prickly ash, Hercules club, yellow Hercules, yellowthorn, yellow prickly ash, sea ash, and pepperwood. Another prickly ash, *Z. americanum*, grows farther north, and is said to be as good. It too was called the toothache tree or toothache bush. For a toothache dry the inner bark, powder it, and apply in the aching tooth cavity.

A strong bark tea was made from the gray dogwood, *Cornus racemosa*, which was held in the mouth to ease the pain of a sore tooth. A root infusion of spotted cranesbill, *Geranium maculatum*, was prepared for toothache in the same way, also recommended for pyorrhea.

The prairie coneflower called gray-headed coneflower, *Ratibida pinnata*, has a root which was said to cure a toothache if you can find it. The rootlets or root hairs of skunk cabbage, *Symplocarpus foetidus*, were another remedy; and it is not surprising that leaves of yarrow, *Achillea millefolium*, were also for toothache besides earaches and other pains.

Dried hops, *Humulus lupulus*, were placed in a small bag and held against the jaw as another remedy. Flaxseed, *Linum lewisii*, could be substituted for hops.

Ground chestnut, *Castanea dentata*, mixed with mutton tallow is said to be good for toothache if you have nothing better. In days when no dentists existed, any toothache remedy must have been a godsend.

COMA, FAINTING, OR CONVULSIONS

As long as we know where there is wild mint, *Mentha arvensis*, we may as well gather a few extra leaves in case we have a feeling of faintness or nausea. No tea for faintness, if you please. Chew the leaves raw, swallow, and see if you aren't perked up considerably. Confidentially, we like the tea best, but if you want to try the raw leaves there is nothing to stop you. Either the peppermint or the Canada mint will do.

The smoke treatment seems to have been accepted for fainting and epileptic convulsions with some plants. The cow parsnip, *Heracleum lanatum*, is obvious in its elephantine leaves along the small watercourses. One burned the tops and inhaled the smoke. It certainly ought to revive most anything.

Another smoke reviver was made by burning the seed pod of the Virginia anemone or thimbleweed, *Anemone virginiana*, in the close vicinity of the patient.

It was said that if you have smooth aster, *Aster laevis*, you should burn the entire plant to furnish smoke while your patient is having a sweat bath to revive him, or if he has lost consciousness you can go to the extreme of forcing smoke from the smoldering smooth aster into his nostrils by a paper cone. Several other asters were used in the same way, including the white heath aster, *A. ericoides*; New England aster, *A. novae-angliae*; willow-leaved aster, *A. salicifolius*; and calico aster, *A. lateriflorus*. The smoked blossoms of the calico aster were considered strong enough medicine to cure even a crazy person.

The bark of the gray dogwood, *Cornus racemosa*, was smudged as a reviver of less potency. Sometimes they burned the white snakeroot, *Eupatorium rugosum*, or else threw it in the sweat bath, whether they called it that or Indian sanicle, richweed, stevia, white sanicle, or deerwort boneset.

If one suffered a stroke of paralysis, he could be revived by allowing him to inhale the sweet-scented smoke of the dried flowers of pearly everlasting, *Anaphalis margaritacea*; the dried petals were powdered and thrown on live coals.

Another plant called many-headed everlasting or mouse-ear everlasting, *Gnaphalium obtusifolium*, was more properly called the fragrant life everlasting. Smoke from the leaves was blown

Smooth aster
Aster laevis

85

Eastern arborvitae branch
Thuja occidentalis

Eastern arborvitae sapling
Thuja occidentalis

into the nostrils to revive one who was fainting, to revive consciousness, or even to bring back loss of mind. Its several names included sweet cudweed, sweet balsam, white balsam, featherweed, and rabbit tobacco.

Perhaps an easier one to find would be the white spruce tree, *Picea glauca*, the needles of which were smoked as an inhalant or a fumigator. Needles of the jack pine, *Pinus banksiana*, could be smoked as a reviver, too. If someone was actually unconscious, they mixed the dried pulverized root of the small Solomon's seal, *Polygonatum biflorum*, with the twigs and leaves of the cedar balm (unidentified botanically), and burned the mixture near the unconscious one to revive him.

The elm-leaved goldenrod, *Solidago ulmifolia*, could be

smudged to revive an unconscious person by directing the smoke up his nostrils; or burn leaves of arborvitae, *Thuja occidentalis*, near the unconscious one. Surely one plant or another might be growing near the emergency.

A smudge was made from the false Solomon's seal, *Smilacina racemosa*, as a reviver after a severe illness. The smoke must have had a sedative effect, because it was said that it would hush a crying child who breathed it, or it would calm one in the throes of a fit or insanity.

As our Victorian grandmothers used smelling salts, their more primitive brothers and sisters made a fainting remedy from the pulverized dried roots of two strangely assorted plants, either but not necessarily both. The Kentucky coffee tree, *Gymnocladus dioica*, the early-shedding and late-leafing tree that makes so pleasant a lawn tree, had considerable power in its roots. Settlers found that its pulverized roots had the faculty of causing uncontrollable sneezing even when a person was in coma, thus being an extreme remedy in reviving such a person.

More mild in its reaction was the pulverized dry root of the bush morning glory, *Ipomoea leptophylla*. If a young lady was subject to fainting spells, not coma, she was often advised to dust the bush morning glory root over her body. One wonders at such a simple remedy, and at an early name for the plant— manroot. Perhaps it had as much effect as the more recent folk belief that a piece of brown wrapping paper worn over the chest will keep a person from getting carsick.

The dried leaves or needles of the white pine, *Pinus strobus*, were powdered and inhaled by one who needed reviving. The ground pine or ground cedar leaves, *Lycopodium complanatum*, were dried in a like manner.

White frontiersmen gathered the buds of the quaking aspen, *Populus tremuloides*, as a stimulant. They seem to have made a beverage of the buds, but the exact directions have escaped us.

The root of the wild sarsaparilla, *Aralia nudicaulis*, made a stimulating tea when one needed it; or you could simmer a leaf tea from sweet fern, *Comptonia peregrina*.

The leaves of the balsam fir, *Abies balsamea*, were thrown in warm bath water in which the patient was immersed to revive him.

87

Mental illness was tackled in various ways in the early days, but when a patient was in the throes of lunacy he was sometimes fed the wax from Kentucky coffee tree pods as a cure—a practice which one questions when one reads that the same wax was a fly poison.

Another belief was that one could stop insanity if a piece of root gum from prairie or western spiderwort, *Tradescantia occidentalis*, were inserted in a cut in the head. If that failed, you could boil the twigs of frost grape, *Vitis vulpina*, and drink the tea.

The root of any of the anemones, *Anemone* spp., was boiled to help paralysis, though it was generally agreed that anemone brew didn't really have much effect, good or bad.

Fits, regardless of what caused them, sometimes reacted favorably to a root tea made from self-heal or heal-all, *Prunella vulgaris*. If not, they were treated by dosing the afflicted one with a root tea from purple coneflower, *Echinacea angustifolia*.

If the patient was strong enough to eat, chewing the roots of white vervain, *Verbena urticaefolium*, would help him.

A patient near death was urged to eat the root of the white baneberry, *Actaea pachypoda*, as a possible reviver, though why one should give a violent purge to someone near death is difficult to understand. If that did not revive him, powdered leaves of spotted bee balm, *Monarda punctata*, were blown into his nostrils.

Old men sometimes took the purple rocket, *Iodanthus pinnatifidus*, to make a plant poultice placed on the head, in the belief that it would bring warmth to the whole body.

DISORDERS OF
STOMACH AND
BOWELS

*T*he believers in these early plant remedies were not too specific about their illnesses, but if they had a stomach ache they had a stomach ache, and there are all kinds of plants that could be found for such vagaries. The pain in the middle has accumulated more folklore plant remedies than any other problem in the body, with the possible exception of childbirth.

Some of the plants are listed in old reports simply as being good for stomach or bowel trouble, with no attempt at any specific description. The poke milkweed, *Asclepias exaltata*, is one such plant. The milkweed family is many and varied, and since the prescription for poke milkweed adds that one must eat the raw root it would be well to carry a botanical handbook to identify this species before taking a nibble. The root of the swamp milkweed, *Asclepias incarnata*, and a large dose of tea from the root of the butterfly weed, *A. tuberosa*, were both general purges.

The pretty cream-colored pea, *Lathyrus ochroleucus*, was picked for an indefinite stomach trouble, but we do not know whether one ate the leaves, root, or possibly the blossom. You can eat the root of the red baneberry, *Actaea rubra*, for

Red baneberry
Actaea rubra

generalized stomach trouble and be well purged with its eating. Red baneberry may be more familiar to you as coral-and-pearl, redberry, snakeroot, poisonberry, snakeberry, toadroot, herb christopher, or grapewort.

Try a leaf tea made from pipsissewa, *Chimaphila umbellatum*, for something milder.

Unidentified internal pains may lessen if you eat the bark of the American sycamore or American plane tree, *Platanus occidentalis*. The fruits of the hops, *Humulus lupulus*, made a fine drink for helping stomach pains. Indeed there are those today who will echo the praises of the hops.

If you have only a mild case of indigestion, it might be better to try a tea steeped from the tops of the Virginia mountain mint, *Pycnanthemum virginianum*; or for a simple stomach ache

Late goldenrod
Solidago gigantea var. *leiophylla*

Canada goldenrod
Solidago canadensis

drink tea from the inner bark of the eastern hemlock tree, *Tsuga canadensis*.

German camomile, *Matricaria chamomilla*, whether called wild camomile or horse gowan, was also brewed for indigestion. As its name implies, German camomile was an import from Europe, maybe brought by immigrants just for medicine.

Several goldenrods were valued for intestinal disorders — Canada goldenrod leaves, *Solidago canadensis*; the fragrant or grassleaf goldenrod, *S. graminifolia*, called bushy goldenrod and flat-topped goldenrod; or the November or late goldenrod, *S. gigantea* var. *leiophylla*.

The root of the cow parsnip, *Heracleum lanatum*, was boiled and drunk for that twinging stomach, or the boiled roots of the burdocks, *Arctium minus* and *A. lappa*, would do. Collected in

91

the autumn, burdock roots were kept through the winter to be convenient as an emetic when needed. Burdocks are easy to see, growing from three to seven feet tall with huge lower leaves. Their popular names include cockle button, cuckold dock, beggar's buttons, hurr-bur, stick-button, hardock, and bardane.

The root of the Canada wild ginger, *Asarum canadense*, fresh or dried, was good for the stomach or as a general mild tonic when mixed with other plants.

The root of the black sampson or purple coneflower, *Echinacea angustifolia*, treated stomach cramps; or grate the root of wake-robin, *Trillium grandiflorum*, and steep and drink as a tea. The dried rhizome of the purple trillium, *Trillium erectum*, made an emetic recognized in pharmacy handbooks. The root of the big bellwort, *Uvularia grandiflora*, was another general stomach remedy.

Stomach cramps were believed to be helped if you boiled and drank a tea from blue-eyed grass, *Sisyrinchium* spp. Both the white blue-eyed grass, *S. albidium*, and the prairie blue-eyed grass, *S. campestre*, were good.

Root tea from bog valerian, *Valeriana uliginosa*, helped cramps, causing warmth in the stomach and a quickening of the pulses if dosed correctly, but large amounts could cause nausea as well. Cramps could be alleviated by a decoction from dried pill-bearing spurge, *Euphorbia pilulifera*. For just plain strengthening the stomach, find the leaves of the plantain-leaved pussytoes, *Antennaria plantaginifolia*, or the white flowers of the pearly everlasting, *Anaphalis margaritacea*, though we cannot say whether you should eat them raw as you find them or make a tea.

Boil the leaves of fragrant cudweed, *Gnaphalium obtusifolium*, the resinous buds of the balm of Gilead poplar, X *Populus gileadensis*, or its cousin the southern poplar, *Populus deltoides* var. *missouriensis*.

If you don't care what happens, they say the poisonous monkshood, *Aconitum papellus*, will excite stomach action when taken judiciously. Keep in mind, however, that it is definitely poison. You will feel the numbness and tingling when it touches your tongue or lips. It isn't worth it.

There are around 250 species of willow known to exist, and

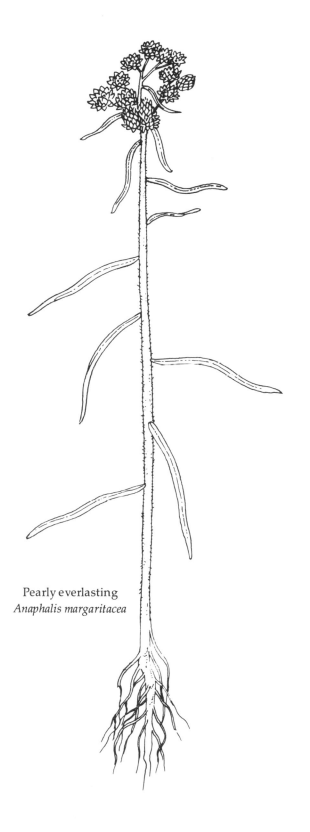

Pearly everlasting
Anaphalis margaritacea

Monkshood
Aconitum sp.

while it is possible that Indian tribes simmered whatever willow was available in their neighborhoods, several species have been definitely identified as ones combatting stomach or bowel disorders. The bark of brittle willow, *Salix fragilis*, called crack willow, was a stomach medicine of mild properties. The root of the prairie or dwarf willow, *S. humilis*, made a tea for either an internal medication or a rectal injection. The shining willow, *S. lucida*, was found in swamps. The bog willow of cold climates, *S. pedicellaris*, and another one growing in swamps, the black willow, *S. nigra*, were accepted.

Sap from the frost grape vine, *Vitis vulpina*, was thought to be good for stomach and bowel trouble. Indigestion or chronic inflammation of the stomach was treated by tea from the bright-yellow root of goldthread, *Coptis groenlandica*, a low plant that looks like a wild strawberry plant except for its lack of fruit.

Another leaf brew can be made from the horsemint or wild bergamot, *Monarda didyma* and *M. fistulosa*. Throw a few flowers of this heavily scented plant with the leaves, boil together, and drink if you can. Horsemint is either the lavender wild bergamot or bee balm or Oswego tea. the *M. fistulosa* flaunts a lavender blossom and the *M. didyma* is red.

Rose-hip skins were eaten for settling the stomach, the idea being that the skin of the rose hips when eaten would cause itching like piles, which in turn would cure the stomach trouble. The meadow rose, *Rosa blanda*, called smooth, pale, or early wild rose, and the pasture or Carolina rose, *R. carolina*, were particularly recognized.

One not so pretty is the thistle, of which several varieties were searched for stomach ache, cramps, bowel pain, or related complaints. The field thistle, *Cirsium discolor*, the common bull thistle, *C. vulgare*, and the Canada thistle, *C. arvense*, were all good. Popular thistle names are confusing. The field thistle, *C. discolor*, is also known as bull thistle, while the real bull thistle, *C. vulgare*, is sometimes called spear thistle, plume thistle, bank thistle, horse thistle, bell thistle, bird thistle, button thistle, boar thistle, or roadside thistle. The Canada thistle, *C. arvense*, has been named creeping thistle, way thistle, cursed thistle, corn thistle, hard thistle, and prickly thistle.

The prairie ground-cherry, *Physalis lanceolata*, growing on

Leaves of willow
Salix sp.

American bugleweed
Lycopus americanus

Field thistle
Cirsium discolor

Creeping hollygrape
Mahonia repens

prairies and waste places through the central plains, and the clammy ground-cherry, *P. heterophylla*, are others that keep their virtues in their roots. The prairie ground-cherry is a hairy-leaved perennial which holds its fruits in a bell-shaped calyx. Having dug the root, simmer it gently and drink for stomach trouble.

Make a root brew of the spikenard, *Aralia racemosa*, if you would rather. The American bugleweed or water horehound plant, *Lycopus americanus*, was mixed with others for plain stomach cramps. You can call the American bugleweed cut-leaved water horehound, gipsywort, or bitter bugle; it is an unassuming little flower that is slow to catch the eye.

If you want a stomach tonic and blood purifier with laxative qualities all thrown in one, make a bark tea from the roots of Oregon grape, *Mahonia aquifolium*, or creeping mahonia, *M. repens*. Either will do the job.

The white sagebrush, *Artemisia gnaphalodes*, made another

Prairie sagebrush
Artemisia frigida

tea. Boil the root and drink. This gray-green plant is called the
western mugwort, and its pungent scent fills the air in many
places west of the Missouri River. The prairie sagebrush, *A.
frigida*, is much prettier from an aesthetic standpoint, and was
a mild cathartic. The St. Louis sagebrush, also called western
mugwort, *A. ludoviciana*, was a generalized digestive ailment
remedy.

A root tea for stomach trouble steeped from the crested
woodfern, *Dryopteris cristata*, was liked by some Indian tribes
but regarded as dangerous by whites. There seemed to be no
worries attached to root tea made from wild cucumber or wild
balsam apple, *Echinocystis lobata*, a medicine known as a purgative for the stomach. The roots of self-heal or heal-all, *Prunella
vulgaris*, were steeped to settle the stomach, lessen stomach
cramps, and generally be good for you.

Stomach trouble may be stomach trouble, but even in olden
days there were times when the mother of a family of sick

99

Cinquefoil
Potentilla sp.

children could say exactly what kind of illness was bothering them. Constipation called for laxatives, and there were many from which to choose.

Teas made from boneset, *Eupatorium perfoliatum*, and horehound, *Marrubium vulgare*, were laxative when taken in large amounts. In a warm infusion, the boneset tea also acted as an emetic to cause vomiting from an upset stomach. Boneset is known by many names—thoroughwort, thorough-stem, thoroughwax, wood boneset, agueweed, feverwort, sweating plant, crosswort, vegetable antimony, tearal, and wild isaac.

Two gentle physics were the seeds of the wild senna, *Cassia marylandica*, soaked in water; and root tea from evening campion, *Lychnis alba*. Some called the *Lychnis* white campion, evening lychnis, snakeflower, thunder flower, bull rattle, cow rattle, or white robin. Another simple laxative was made from leaves of the giant St.-John's-wort, *Hypericum ascyron*.

If you take bogbean tea, *Menyanthes trifoliata*, in small quantities it will act as a mild purge. If you take a real swig of the brew it will induce vomiting in no mean proportions. Call it buckbean, marsh trefoil, bean trefoil, water trefoil, bitter trefoil, water shamrock, moonflower, marsh clover, bitterworm, bognut, or brook bean.

Broad-leaved plantain, *Plantago major*, can be steeped for a medicine for general bowel troubles if you cannot find the bogbean, and dandelion tea would be even easier to find. The dandelion, *Taraxacum officinale*, was good for lots of things, including a laxative, the liver, indigestion, constipation — but you must boil the root for this.

The *Silphium* species were convenient too. A soothing laxative came from the boiled root of the rosinweed, *S. integrifolium*, and the compass plant, *S. laciniatum*. General stomach trouble needed root tea from the cup rosinweed or cup plant, *S. perfoliatum*, and one could chew the gum from the stem to keep from vomiting.

One of the mildest laxatives, and therefore probably for children as well as adults, was made from boiling the root of the pitcher plant, *Sarracenia purpurea*. On the other hand, for chronic constipation it was suggested that a root tea be brewed from silverleaf scurf pea, *Psoralea argophylla*.

100

Two nut trees were valued for their medical properties as physics. The sap of the butternut, *Juglans cinerea*, was boiled to syrup stage, though the butternut twigs and roots could be boiled for an emetic too. The inner bark of the black walnut, *J. nigra*, was boiled to make a strong or mild physic depending on the intensity of the brew. It was as good a medicine for dysentery.

The root of the drug sweet flag, also called calamus root, *Acorus calamus*, was a good physic when boiled, though one was cautioned to take it only in small doses. Another which must be taken carefully in small quantities was the yellow wild indigo, *Baptisia tinctoria*. The dried root was a good purge when used properly, but remember — only a minimum dose. Both root and leaves of the wild indigo, *Baptisia leucantha*, were sometimes combined with other plants. By itself, *B. leucantha* was an intestinal stimulant to be taken only in small doses, too, a root-leaf tea for dysentery, a laxative and emetic. Similarly, a little root tea from small Solomon's seal, *Polygonatum biflorum*, was good for the digestion, but increase the amount and it becomes a physic. You must go easy until you know how much to take.

Two varieties of cinquefoil could be a physic when you have cramps in the stomach. The entire plant was steeped if you have rough cinquefoil, *Potentilla norvegica*, also called barren strawberry, but you should use only the swamp root of the marsh cinquefoil, *Potentilla palustris*, also called marsh five-finger, purple cinquefoil, purple marshlock, cowberry, purplewort, and meadownuts.

A strong physic was that made from Culver's physic, *Veronicastrum virginicum*, for chronic constipation as cathartic or emetic, and thought by some to be a remedy in duodenal indigestion.

A physic was brewed from the inner bark of either the European snowball tree, *Viburnum opulus*, or the highbush cranberry, *V. trilobum*, said to be good for cramps or all-over body pains.

Boil the whole plant of rosy twisted-stalk, *Streptopus roseus*, for a physic, or boil the bark of the alder buckthorn, *Rhamnus alnifolia*. The alder buckthorn is also known as alder-leaved buckthorn and dwarf alder.

Twisted-stalk
Streptopus roseus

101

Snowball tree
Viburnum opulus

Pokeweed
Phytolacca americana

Standish honeysuckle
Lonicera Standishii

Settlers steeped the stem bark of the wahoo, *Euonymus atropurpurea*, for a medicine that could be a drastic purge if taken in large quantities, or a mild laxative in small doses.

A good laxative was a tea from the wood of black ash, *Fraxinus nigra*, mixed with the root of *Smilax racemosa*, though black-ash bark alone was steeped for vague internal ailments. The entire plant of butter-and-eggs toadflax, *Linaria vulgaris*, was boiled, All varieties of the honeysuckle, *Lonicera* spp., made purges, both as emetic and cathartic, although the American fly honeysuckle, *Lonicera canadensis*, was considered best. Another purge that acted both as emetic and cathartic was a strong dosage of the root of horse gentian, *Triosteum perfoliatum*.

That startling blue blossom the blue flag, *Iris versicolor*, made a root tea well known as a physic. The plant is so obvious when blooming that it has gathered a number of names, including iris, flag lily, liver lily, snake lily, poison flag, water flag, American fleur-de-lis, and flower-de-luce.

Several emetics were made from wild plants that afterward found their way into early pharmacy handbooks. *Apocynum androsaemifolium*, the spreading dogbane, was one; the dried rhizome and roots were mentioned as a purge but with a caution to the druggist to use only with care.

If one wanted to modify the action of purgatives, it was said that dried ripe fruit of fennel, *Foeniculum vulgare*, would serve the purpose, and volatile oil prepared from fennel would also act against gas on the stomach.

Pokeweed, *Phytolacca americana*, was known to be a violent emetic, and prescribed occasionally even though it was also a dangerous drug, sometimes causing death. A more common agent to cause vomiting was the ripe seeds of white, yellow, or black mustard, respectively *Brassica hirta*, *B. alba*, and *B. nigra*. These were also cultivated, so may have been kept in the cupboard for the purpose.

An emetic known from early times is the brew made from the rootstock of button snakeroot, *Eryngium aquaticum*. This plant of several popular names can grow six feet high under favorable conditions, making it easy to spot.

We find one berry eaten for stomach trouble, that of the American bittersweet, *Celastrus scandens*. The berries were not

American bittersweet
Celastrus scandens

Blue vervain
Verbena stricta

gathered for food as many berries were, but were reserved for their medicinal properties. They were an emetic, though they also caused increased perspiration with the taking. Modern pharmaceutical handbooks warn against haphazard dosage of the berry because of its undependability.

A warm infusion of the root of purple-stem angelica, *Angelica atropurpurea*, carries no such warning with its medication. Another emetic was simmered from the inner bark of the buttonbush, *Cephalanthus occidentalis*. Buttonbush has several names—button tree, honeyballs, globeflower, buttonwood shrub, box, pinball, little snowball, button willow, crane willow, swampwood, riverbush, and crouper bush.

Bracken, *Pteridium aquilinum*, made a root tea that had its followers for stomach cramps or in large doses for a purgative. Bloodroot, *Sanguinaria canadensis*, is recognized today as a plant that stimulates gastric juices in the stomach in very small doses, but if the amount is too strong it will cause vomiting, muscular prostration, fainting, and even death.

The bark of black locust, *Robinia pseudocacia*, was accepted by some Indians without qualms, but whites considered it poisonous. It has been known to act on the body as a strong emetic and purge, perhaps stronger than the average frontiersmen liked. Officially called black locust, it is also known as white, yellow, or green locust, locust tree, false acacia, bastard acacia, peaflower locust, post locust, and silver chain. Livestock have been known to die from eating too much of the bark or young shoots.

Another potent tea was made from the root of the low poppy mallow, *Callirrhoë involucrata*, called purple mallow or purple poppy mallow. One didn't find the low poppy mallow in great quantities on the plains and still cannot, but if you search it is there. This showy flower may have been picked almost to extinction, as so often happens when a brilliant blossom is its own undoing. Its rose-purple bloom grows from one to three inches wide, flaunting its color like a banner.

The blue verbena, *Verbena stricta*, is easy to see wherever it grows, too. Some know it as wild verbena, blue vervain, verbain, false verbain, or simpler's joy. The indecisive flowering of the tall stalks scatters its blue down moist valleys and draws over the United States. We need not bother the roots of the blue verbena. Just pick the leaves, boil, and drink to settle that churning stomach — or simmer the flowering tops as an emetic. Another emetic was made from boiling the whole plant of the bedstraw or cleavers, *Galium aparine*.

The Indian tobacco lobelia, *Lobelia inflata*, was known as a violent emetic to the extent that several of its popular names were built on that trait. It was called gagroot, emetic weed, vomitwort, pukeweed, and emetic herb, besides asthma weed, wild tobacco, bladderpod, low belia, and eyebright. Though it is recognized as poisonous if misused, when handled correctly it had its medical followers. In spite of the emetic quality of the leaves, it is said that the juices of the fruit acted as an anti-spasmodic.

The elder trees were treated carefully as medication for stomach and bowel upsets. While the dried blossoms of the blueberry elder, *Sambucus cerulea*, made a tea that soothed the stomach, the steeped inner bark made a strong emetic that caused vomiting. The elderberry, *S. canadensis*, is the best known of the common elder bushes, and has acquired several familiar names — sweet elder, elder flowers, and elder blows. Even young twigs of the elderberry have an inner bark which is a strong purgative, and the wise man will not take the root of the American elder internally in any form, though the bark of the root can be adapted very carefully for some medications. The red-berried elder, *S. pubens*, was reserved for very stubborn or extreme cases of serious constipation. Menomini Indians in Wisconsin made a brew from red-berried elder inner bark and rind which they knew to be a drastic purge or powerful emetic, but they prescribed it with the greatest of care and minimum dose. Whites of early days were inclined to leave red-berried elder inner bark strictly alone, believing it to produce death if eaten. The berries were reputed to be poisonous, although they have not been proved to be. The shrub has been called poison elder, boor tree, bore tree, and boutry.

Skunk cabbage, *Symplocarpus foetidus*, was valued in many ways. The root was boiled for cramps in various proportions to cause vomiting or to ease vomiting. Large amounts caused vomiting with the added misery of a headache, and as a result the drug was avoided when other medicines were available. Folks have known it as skunkweed, polecat weed, swamp

Oxeye daisy
Chrysanthemum leucanthemum

Fruit of red elderberry
Sambucus pubens

Blossom of red elderberry
Sambucus pubens

cabbage, meadow cabbage, collard, fetid hellebore, stinking poke, or pockweed. On one point they all agree—it smells bad.

Another plant tea, that of oxeye daisy, *Chrysanthemum leucanthemum*, was an antispasmodic if taken in small doses but tended to increase vomiting in large doses, the difference between small and large depending on one's sensitivity to the brew. Oxeye daisy is another flower with a host of names, including white daisy, field daisy, dog daisy, bull daisy, butter daisy, big daisy, midsummer daisy, moon daisy, horse daisy, poorland daisy, maudlin daisy, dutch morgan, moonpenny, great white oxeye, poverty weed, white man's weed, herb margaret, bull's-eye daisy, sheriff-pink, and dog blow.

To settle the stomach and keep from vomiting, one found either the small yellow lady's-slipper, *Cypripedium parviflorum*, or the showy lady's-slipper, *C. reginae*, presumably in a root tea.

Tea from small cranberry, *Vaccinium oxycoccos*, could combat nausea, and had an astringent quality in controlling diarrhea.

When Lewis and Clark followed their exploratory trek into the wilderness and Captain Lewis was cured of a "dysentery and fever"[1] by the chokecherry bush, it was not just happenstance. The black chokecherry or western chokecherry, *Prunus virginiana* var. *melanocarpa*, was known for its healing power by the Indians of that day. The cherry on the bush was edible, but they knew that a decoction of the bark was the thing to drink if one had a touch of diarrhea. Most of the *Prunus* species were stomach-trouble medicines. When nauseated, the stomach was settled by drinking bark tea from the Canada plum tree, *P. nigra*; the bark of the related pin cherry, *P. pensylvanica*, known as wild red cherry; the black cherry, *P. serotina*; and the chokecherry, *P. virginiana*. Chokecherry tea was also good for piles when used as a rectal injection.

It was said that if you had an upset stomach you should scrape the bark downward from a peach tree, boil it, and drink it, and scrape the bark upward if that stomach upset turned into diarrhea. The peach tree, *Prunus persica*, is a southern tree.

---

[1] Maximilian, Prince of Wied, *Travels in the Interior of North America*. Reprinted by Thwaites, Reuben Gold, in *Early Western Travels*. Cleveland: Arthur H. Clark Co., 1906. Vol. 2, pp. 83–84.

Yellow lady's slipper
Cypripedium calceolus var. *parviflorum*

Pin cherry
Prunus pensylvanica

Western chokecherry
Prunus virginiana var. *melanocarpa*

A good purge for summer diarrhea both as a physic and an emetic was made from the root of mayapple, *Podophyllum peltatum*. Alone it could be given to children, but the mayapple or mandrake root tea was made considerably more powerful by adding Jacob's ladder, *Polemonium reptans*, known by some as Greek valerian, bluebell, or sweatroot.

There were other plants that gave their leaves to fight diarrhea symptoms. The silktop dalea, *Dalea aurea*, made a concoction of boiled leaves that was said to cure either colic or dysentery. This plant grew on the plains west of the Missouri River and sometimes crept up the lower foothills.

If one lived east of the Missouri River he would be wiser to look for the tall gayfeather or rough spike gayfeather, *Liatris scariosa*. Some botanists scoff at the name "blazing star" also given the plant as inept and inappropriate to its appearance. Others have referred to it as colicroot, devil's bite, grayfeather, blue blazing star, rattlesnake master, or large button snakeroot. Call it what you will. If we have diarrhea we are not ready to quarrel over a name but will be quite willing to gather the narrow leaves and corm to make our tea and lie back to be cured.

The American water lily, *Nymphaea odorata*, or the root of the yellow pond lily, *Nuphar advena*, was a diarrhea or dysentery medicine used by white settlers, not by the Indians.

A tonic brew for loss of appetite and diarrhea was made from the leaves of yarrow, *Achillea millefolium*, of mild laxative properties. Yarrow leaves are sometimes steeped even in this day for diseased conditions of the gastrointestinal tract, and it is no wonder that the plant has many names. Some know it as milfoil, thousand-leaf, gordaldo, green arrow, soldiers' woundwort, nosebleed, dog daisy, sanguinary, carpenter grass, old-man's-pepper, or cammock.

The leaves and bark of the speckled or hoary alder, *Alnus rugosa*, were boiled by whites to treat diarrhea, but Indians boiled the root of the alder for the purpose.

Yellow sweet clover, *Melilotus officinalis*, is a wide-spreading plant that can cover acres of ground when it once gets started. The dried leaves and tiny flowering tops made a brew for diarrhea, though we are cautioned today that it also has a tendency to develop hemorrhages.

American water lily
Nymphaea odorata

Yellow sweet clover
Melilotus officinalis

You can make a safe tea from the root and leaves of the
pretty wild columbine, *Aquilegia canadensis*, which was good for
diarrhea or most any kind of stomach and bowel troubles.
Having pulled it by the roots, you may as well enjoy the
beauty of the red and yellow blossoms by arranging them as
cut flowers in your living room, though the wild columbine is
harder to find in late years and one would rather leave them in
the woods where they grow.

The bark of the winterberry, *Ilex verticillata*, made a decoction
for diarrhea treatment. Other names were often given the plant

— Virginia winterberry, black alder, feverbush, striped alder, white alder, and false alder. Don't eat the berries; they are poisonous.

Blackberry and raspberry roots were simmered for tonic and astringent properties in combatting summer diarrhea or other bowel upsets. Those particularly sought for this purpose were the mountain blackberry, *Rubus allegheniensis*; the blackcap raspberry, *R. occidentalis*; the American red raspberry, *R. idaeus* var. *strigosus*; and the western red raspberry, *R. idaeus* var. *aculeatissimus*. The mountain blackberry also made a blackberry cordial said to be good for summer diarrhea. As late as 1877 one could read advertisements in the newspaper such as this which appeared in the *Black Hills Daily Times*, June 28, 1877:

Blackberry Brandy (pure juice) for summer complaints at Morton's Club House.[2]

"Summer complaint" was the polite term for diarrhea at the time, and there wasn't the slightest doubt in anyone's mind when they read the ad as to what it meant.

The bark of the American beech, *Fagus grandifolia*, was valued in the same way; or a tea from mayweed, *Anthemis cotula*. Mayweed could be more familiar to you in one of its popular names: dog's camomile, fetid camomile, dillweed, mather, dog fennel, hog's fennel, dog finkle, morgan, dog daisy, pigsty daisy, maise, chigger weed, or balders.

Dysentery was occasionally treated by the dried whole plants of some violets, *Viola* spp. If you developed loose bowels by eating strange foods, you could be helped by chewing pine pitch from the western yellow or ponderosa pine, *Pinus ponderosa*, or by boiling the needles of the same tree for a medicinal tea.

Use the roots of white rattlesnake root, *Prenanthes alba*; of the purple gerardia, *Gerardia tenuifolia*; or the Virginia creeper, *Parthenocissus quinquefolia*. The delicate sweet fern, *Comptonia peregrina*, was gathered to make a leaf tea strong enough to cure the flux and stomach cramps. The plant has several popular names, including ferngale, fern bush, meadow fern,

[2]*Black Hills Daily Times*, Deadwood, South Dakota. June 28, 1877, advertisement.

117

Ponderosa pine
Pinus ponderosa

Virginia creeper
Parthenocissus quinquefolia

shrubby fern, Canada sweet gale, spleenwort bush, sweet
bush, and sweet ferry, and can be found growing from one to
three feet high.

A really drastic purgative even stronger than sweet fern was
made from the hedge bindweed, *Convolvulus sepium*. The white
blossoms are of the morning glory family, dainty enough to
form a table decoration as well. They are known as great
bindweed, bellbind, woodbind, pear vine, devil's vine,
lady's-nightcap, Rutland beauty, German scammony, and
bracted bindweed.

119

Hedge bindweed
Convolvulus sepium

A diarrhea medicine was the root of the canaigre, *Rumex hymenosepalus*, one of the docks. Its tuberous roots contain tannin needed in the treatment of leather. That might be comforting when one is thinking of stomach diseases. A leather stomach might be more resistant to illnesses.

When dysentery was accompanied by abdominal bloating, the thing to do was to abrade the surface of the abdomen and apply pulverized dried leaves of one of the spurges, the thyme-leaved spurge, *Euphorbia serpyllifolia*. If you find the flowering spurge instead, *E. corollata*, pound a half-inch of the root, boil in water, and drink a cupful before breakfast. It was considered an excellent laxative or cathartic, either alone or with other roots. In the memory of some old-timers the root juice was once an emetic, but it has been abandoned for that purpose. It has been known as blooming spurge, apple root, bowman's root, purging root, picac, milk purslane, white purslane, milk pusley, milk ipecac, milkweed, snake milk, and wild hippo. All *Euphorbia* species can raise blisters on susceptible people, and an overdose of the root tea can make anyone mighty sick.

Dysentery was attacked by a medicine made from the brownish-purple-flowered hound's-tongue, *Cynoglossum officinale*, a plant known as beggar's-lice. A purge both as an emetic and a cathartic was effective when made from the fruit of the dwarf bush honeysuckle, *Diervilla lonicera*; and the leaves of the little bearberry, *Arctostaphylos uva-ursi*, were steeped in a tea.

For women severely ill with diarrhea, boil the seeds of Nuttall's prairie parsley, *Polytaenia nuttalli*, for a medicine to be drunk. When even bleeding in the bowels occurred, it was treated by a brew made by boiling the bright berries of the smooth sumac, *Rhus glabra*; but if the illness was only simple inward troubles, as they were sometimes vaguely called, a root bark tea was made from staghorn sumac, *R. typhina*. The inner bark of the trunk rather than the root bark made an infusion good for shrinking piles or stopping internal hemorrhages as a rectal injection.

The root and leaves of hardhack, *Spiraea tomentosa*, were an astringent tonic to combat diarrhea, hemorrhages, or ulcers in the intestines. For a blood flux, the immature seeds of the meadowsweet, *Spiraea alba*, made an internal medicine; or a solution made from the small skullcap, *Scutellaria parvula*. For flux in children or excessive fluid discharge from bowels, some soaked the leaves and stems of the bigroot lady's thumb, or swamp persicaria, *Polygonum coccineum*, using cold water. The decoction has an astringent action that also allayed accompanying stomach pains. The Pennsylvania persicaria or smartweed, *Polygonum pensylvanicum*, was good for bloody flux and beneficial for piles.

For internal pains of indeterminate origin, especially if there were signs of internal bleeding, our forefathers boiled the stems of the Atlantic coreopsis or tall tickseed, *Coreopsis tripteris*, and drank the liquid.

Hedge bindweed
Convolvulus sepium

121

Spiraea
cultivated *Spiraea* sp.

Smartweed
Polygonum pennsylvanicum

Scouring rush
Equisetum hyemale

An astringent rectal injection was brewed from the stems of scouring rush, *Equisetum hyemale*; the annual fleabane plant, *Erigeron annuus*, that small white daisylike blossom with tinges of purple on the rays sometimes called sweet scabious, white top, or lace buttons; the horseweed fleabane, *Erigeron canadensis*; or the bark of American hornbeam or blue beech, *Carpinus caroliniana*. A liquid rectal injection was made from the bark of silky dogwood, *Cornus amomum*, for diarrhea, and a like remedy was made for piles by steeping the bark of pagoda dogwood or alternate-leaved dogwood, *C. alternifolia*, or the bark tea of gray dogwood, *C. racemosa*.

123

Tannic acid is found too in the inner bark of the white oak, *Quercus alba*, sometimes known as stone oak or stave oak. An infusion of white oak bark was made by white settlers of the west as an astringent rectal injection for piles, or for settling diarrhea symptoms.

Pulverized dried root of the Kentucky coffee tree, *Gymnocladus dioica*, was mixed with water to form an enema solution.

The alumroots, rough alumroot, *Heuchera hispida*, and American alumroot, *H. americana*, made a very good astringent rectal injection; and the Virginia waterleaf, *Hydrophyllum virginianum*, had similar properties. A soothing rectal injection for intestinal disorders was steeped from the roots of fireweed, *Epilobium angustifolium*, or great willow herb, a brew that had a tonic effect on any mucous surface. The glade mallow, *Napaea dioica*, was prescribed for piles too.

Another astringent rectal injection to heal piles, diarrhea, flux, hemorrhoids, or weak intestinal muscles was made from the root of the wild geranium, *Geranium maculatum*. The wild geranium is known by many names — cranesbill, spotted cranesbill, wild cranesbill, storksbill, chocolate flower, crow-foot, dove's-foot, old-maid's-nightcap, and shameface. Besides boiling the geranium root in an infusion, the root was sometimes pounded to be a poultice for protruding piles. The root tea was considered good when drunk for a delicate stomach. Mixed with bark of the white oak, *Quercus alba*, the florets of purple prairie clover, *Petalostemon purpureus*, it was another diarrhea medicine.

On the other hand, a medicine made from the root of the American wood anemone, *Anemone quinquefolia*, was valuable in many ways except for the stomach, it being said that if one drank anemone tea it would cause inflammation of the stomach and intestines.

From our collection of medicinal plants already mentioned, we have several that can counteract gas pains as well as other needs. We have noted thyme-leaved spurge, *Euphorbia serpyllifolia*, supposed to be fine for dysentery. The thyme leaf was also used for plain abdominal bloating; the surface of the abdomen was abraded and pulverized dried leaves were applied.

124

Rough alum root
Heuchera hispida

Prairie clover
Petalostemon purpureus

Wild mint
Mentha arvensis var. *villosa*

If there were any buffalo left on the plains we could secure some buffalo fat and mix it with the pulverized seeds of the cream-colored false indigo, *Baptisia leocophaea*, to make a penetrating salve to rub on the abdomen. This member of the pea family is also called the black rattlepod.

The calamus root or sweet flag, *Acorus calamus*, and the silktop dalea, *Dalea aurea*, were found to make a tea for colic. While the silktop dalea must be picked for its leaves and the leaves steeped, the calamus root made a more potent beverage by boiling the pounded root stock.

The tops and leaves of the curlycup gumweed, *Grindelia*

Catnip
Nepeta cataria

Caraway
Carum carvi

squarrosa, called gum plant, sticky-heads, broad-leaved gum plant, or scaly grindelia, could be boiled for a colic cure. This plant is common on dry plains. We remember as a child picking the sticky yellow blooms of the plant to affix to the tip of our fingers. There was no reason for this as we recall, but children seldom need a reason other than delight.

The entire plant, leaves and tops, made a colic remedy when one found the sweet fern, *Comptonia peregrina*.

Of all the teas that treat gas on the stomach, we can think of none more pleasant than that of Canada mint, *Mentha arvensis* var. *villosa*, the common names of which include wild mint and

127

American mint. Peppermint, *Mentha piperita*, is also called American mint as well as brandy mint, lamb mint, or lammint, and is used the same way. The mints grow easily over the plains states wherever there is enough moisture to encourage them, and their dark-green leaves are a deep color against a white house in many a small town. Pluck the young and tender leaves, steep them in hot water for a few minutes, and drink with a dash of sugar. This may be good for colic, but it can be served just for pleasure, too. We do not believe that anyone has ever been harmed by a cup of wild mint tea.

Other fairly safe teas could be made from thyme, *Thymus vulgaris*, the dried tops collected when the plant was in flower; from caraway, the dried fruit of *Carum carvi*; or the dried ripe fruit of the anise, *Pimpinella anisum*. The lovely flowering dogwood, *Cornus florida*, was dug for its dried root bark to make a mild stomach medicine, too.

The root bark of the paper birch, *Betula papyrifera*, was cooked with maple sugar to make a syrup said to alleviate stomach cramps, and probably tasted good as well.

Other commonly known wild teas for stomach disorders were catnip tea, *Nepeta cataria*, and camomile tea, *Matricaria chamomilla*. Catnip tea was given even to colicky babies.

One of the foods eaten in early days was said to settle the stomach as well as being good eating. This was the toothwort, *Dentaria maxima*, which was cooked with corn after a fermentation process.

Sometimes a popular name of a plant gives the clue to what its value once was. The white-tube star grass, *Aletris farinosa*, was known as colicroot. Other familiar names for the stargrass were blazing star, mealy starwort, unicorn root, unicorn's horn, devil's bit, ague grass, ague root, aloeroot, crow corn, and huskroot.

Another root tea for colic or gas was made from swamp milkweed, *Asclepias incarnata*, or from butterfly weed, *Asclepias tuberosa*, if taken in small quantities.

If you are sick enough to be able to say you are suffering with bilious colic, then perhaps you need a decoction of the roots of the yam, *Dioscorea villosa*. For just plain getting rid of too much gas, wintergreen, *Gaultheria procumbens*, known by many names, was accepted fairly widely as a leaf tea.

Paper birch
Betula papyrifera

Wild bergamot, bee balm, or horsemint, *Monarda fistulosa*, offered its leaves and flowers for a tea to combat colic, nausea, vomiting, generally settling the stomach. The spotted bee balm, *Monarda punctata*, was all right too, but worked better when combined with other plants.

The roots of the prairie willow, *Salix humilis*, called dwarf willow, were said to make a good colic medicine.

The leaves of Canada goldenrod, *Solidago canadensis*, made a mild carminative for gas on the stomach, as did those of the November or late goldenrod, *S. gigantea* var. *leiophylla*, and the grassleaf goldenrod, *S. graminifolia*.

The inner bark of maple-leaved viburnum, *Viburnum acerifolium*, made a tea to relieve cramps caused by intestinal gas. Some called it arrowwood, squash berry, maple-leaved guelder rose, or dockmackie.

DISORDERS OF OTHER INTERNAL ORGANS

GLANDS

*E*nlarged glands either did not occur too often in primitive days or they had the frontier intellect stymied. Only a few plants were known for such troubles. One plant, the black sampson or purple coneflower, *Echinacea angustifolia*, is mentioned as being a remedy for such an occurrence. Inasmuch as the purple coneflower was used more or less like our modern miracle drugs, good for nearly everything, the frontier folk might have just been making a shot in the dark.

Various scrofulous conditions were treated by a leaf brew made from pipsissewa, *Chimaphila umbellatum*. Sometimes leatherwood bark, *Dirca palustris*, was combined with wild sarsaparilla, *Aralia nudicaulis*, to make a medicine. Two docks were known for the trouble, the *Rumex crispus*, curled dock, and the *R. obtusifolius*, yellow or bitter dock. Both gave their roots, which were made into a decoction applied locally over the swelling.

The root of burdock, *Arctium minus*, was steeped and drunk; and another tea was made from the small bedstraw, *Galium trifidum*. Blue flag, *Iris versicolor*, was thought to make a good

131

Compass plant
Silphium laciniatum

Curled dock
Rumex crispus

root tea, too; or glandular enlargements were treated by drinking a root tea from the compass plant, *Silphium laciniatum*.

It seems at this distance in time that treating swollen or diseased glands with any kind of wild tea was somewhat risky, but again we must remember the lack of doctors on the frontier. When children were sick, they were sick. Something had to be done. After all, how do we know? Maybe it did have some value.

Some plants we mention have acquired a folklore value primarily by their having been brought by frontiersmen who pushed America's border west, rather than by being used by the Indians who lived on the land before them. Such plants were the red or white baneberries, *Actaea rubra* and *A. pachypoda*, known by whites for heart ailments but for quite a different purpose by the Indians. The root of either was believed to be good for the circulation, and a last resort when one suspected a fatty or irritable heart.

The bark of the red oak, *Quercus rubra*, was thought to be beneficial for the heart, and the false Solomon's seal, *Smilacina racemosa*, was said to strengthen the heart muscle. *S. racemosa* and *S. stellata* look very similar to the casual observer, the difference being most obvious in the berries.

A heart stimulant was made from the root of the Indian hemp, *Apocynum cannabinum*, or the spreading dogbane, *A. androsaemifolium*, by steeping a tea which could also be drunk for other ailments.

When one could find them, the leaves of striped pipsissewa, *Chimaphila maculata*, were brewed for heart disease.

Certain cardiac properties were attributed to hawthorn berries, more often called thorn apples, *Crataegus* spp. One ate the fruit, and believed it to be generally strengthening for the heart. The fruits of pear hawthorn, *Crataegus calpodendron*, were said to be especially valued.

A bright spot of red on the prairies could well be the prairie meadowsweet, *Filipendula rubra*, often called queen of the prairie. Indians gathered it for heart trouble, though they also called it a love medicine. The two references, heart and love, are so intermixed by the inexact that we cannot really tell whether it was wanted for physical heart ailments or not.

The Seneca snakeroot, *Polygala senega*, so highly esteemed for its anti-snakebite properties, was also used for heart trouble by boiling the root and drinking the hot beverage.

Heart palpitation brought on by being highly nervous was treated by the sedative qualities in bark tea from the black cherry, *Prunus serotina*. Heartburn—actually a stomach disorder—suggested meadow rose, *Rosa blanda;* the flowers were

133

Star-flowered false Solomon's seal
Smilacina stellata

dried and powdered, then made into a beverage. A decoction
of the marsh skullcap, *Scutellaria epilobiifolia*, was a heart remedy of general use. Call it hooded willow herb or European
skullcap if you wish. Dandelion, *Taraxacum officinale*, provided
a root tea for heartburn, though some folks preferred a plant
tea made from the lavender American dog violet, *Viola
conspersa*. Others made a brew from the inner bark of the
prickly ash, *Zanthoxylum americana*, for heart disease or to
augment the pulse rate.

The dried leaf of digitalis or purple foxglove, *Digitalis
purpurea*, has always been known as a powerful heart

medicine, slowing or strengthening the heartbeat when taken properly. Digitalis was prescribed in England before America, and doctors depend on it today. It has accumulated over sixty names — thimbles, fairy cup, popdock, rabbit flower, Scotch mercury, and a variety of others simply too numerous to mention.

If digitalis isn't conveniently located, you might substitute the root of small Solomon's seal, *Polygonatum biflorum*, which is less powerful but better than nothing.

KIDNEY OR URINARY SYSTEM

When we find ourselves prescribing for kidney or urinal troubles we begin to feel quite professional, so we hasten to remind you that we are historians only, reporting these old medicines for their folklore value only. If they are interesting it is because they are part of American culture, although many have found their way into modern pharmaceutical handbooks in one way or another.

Having salved our conscience, we may admit that it is a wonder any plants at all are left on the prairies, what with the passion our pioneers had for pulling them by the roots. The wild black currant, *Ribes americanum*, which makes such delicious jelly if allowed to ripen in its fruits, was one that gave its root and its life for medicine. The prairie settlers boiled the root and drank the decoction for kidney trouble. With our mind on the jelly we would so much rather have, we sincerely hope it did them some good.

The root of the false Solomon's seal, *Smilacina racemosa*, was mixed with the rosy-flowered spreading dogbane, *Apocynum androsaemifolium*, as a kidney medicine, though either dogbane, *A. androsaemifolium* or *A. cannabinum*, was valued for the purpose.

The root of the white baneberry, *Actaea pachypoda*, was said to be a good urinary remedy by itself, though it was likely to make you quite sick in the process. You would be wiser to make a root tea from burdock, *Arctium minus*. A milder remedy was a root tea from Canada wild ginger, *Asarum canadense*; or from dwarf bush honeysuckle, *Diervilla lonicera*. Whites picked

Spiderwort
Tradescantia sp.

the fruit of the dwarf bush honeysuckle as well as the root, or combined it with ground pine, *Lycopodium obscurum*.

Chronic kidney trouble was treated by a root tea made from leatherwood, *Dirca palustris*, also called moosewood. It was said that the bark of the bush was as effective, though the bark can be irritating to the skin.

If a very mild medicine was needed, root tea was made from the pitcher plant, *Sarracenia purpurea*. Of course one could always find a dandelion, *Taraxacum officinale*, to make a root tea for urinary troubles. If that is too easy, look for the prairie or western spiderwort, *Tradescantia occidentalis*, for a fine root tea remedy.

The white rattlesnake root, *Prenanthes alba*, also called white lettuce, has a milky juice considered to be a urinary medicine that may have been difficult to obtain in many localities. The

Joe-pye weed
Eupatorium purpureum

root of self-heal or heal-all, *Prunella vulgaris*, probably was better known.

A powerful remedy was that from the roots of mayapple, *Podophyllum peltatum*, and Jacob's ladder, *Polemonium reptans*, boiled together. This is a strong purgative too, and must be taken only in small measured amounts. Too much can be harmful.

The root of small Solomon's seal, *Polygonatum biflorum*, augments the flow of urine to such an extent that it has treated dropsy.

If blood shows in the urine, boil the root of the dotted gayfeather or dotted button snakeroot, *Liatris punctata*, and drink the root tea. The tall gayfeather or blazing star, *Liatris scariosa*, was all right, too.

The root of the giant or great St.-John's-wort, *Hypericum*

pyramidatum, was mixed with the root of the black raspberry, *Rubus occidentalis*, to treat kidney troubles; or find the spotted or corymbed St.-John's-wort, *Hypericum punctatum*, if the great St.-John's-wort is not available.

The root of blue flag, *Iris versicolor*, was said to be good for dropsy and several other ailments. A root tea from Canada wood nettle, *Laportea canadensis*, helps the body hold the urine rather than discharge it. Cloudy urine could be cleared by the root of the blue verbena, *Verbena hastata*; or if the urine is whitish, the root of the ostrich fern, *Pteretis pensylvanica*, was steeped to make a drink that might help.

The roots of the pink-flowered joe-pye weed, *Eupatorium purpureum*, were boiled for diseases of the genitourinary canals, its astringent and diuretic properties acting favorably on various urinary disorders. White snakeroot, *E. rugosum*, was preferred by white settlers for the purpose.

The rootstock of the tall button snakeroot, *Eryngium aquaticum*, made a medicine for bladder trouble. Button snakeroot has several names: eryngo, water eryngo, corn snakeroot, rattlesnake master, and rattlesnake flag. The root of the swamp milkweed, *Asclepias incarnata*, was needed for the dose, or you could boil the root of butterfly weed, *Asclepias tuberosa*.

The pink-flowered smartweed, *Polygonum pensylvanicum*, was gathered as a diuretic in southern states, either the root or leaf being needed.

The root tea of blue cohosh, *Caulophyllum thalictroides*, was valued by early Indian women for various female ailments, by their men as a genitourinary remedy. The greenish-yellow flowers identified the plant but the rootstock with all roots were the medical part needed. It is a dangerous medicine, though.

A plant that flourishes on the floor of some lakes is the brittle stonewort, *Chara fragilis*, an alga, once thought to be good for kidney troubles. The difficulty in obtaining it doubtless made it a plant only rarely prepared.

Another one needed for its root was the smooth sumac, *Rhus glabra*, known as scarlet sumac because of its bright coloring in the autumn. Make a drink of the root, boil, strain, and gulp.

The root of the giant hyssop, *Agastache scrophulariaefolia*, made a similar tea. The root of the agrimony, *Agrimonia*

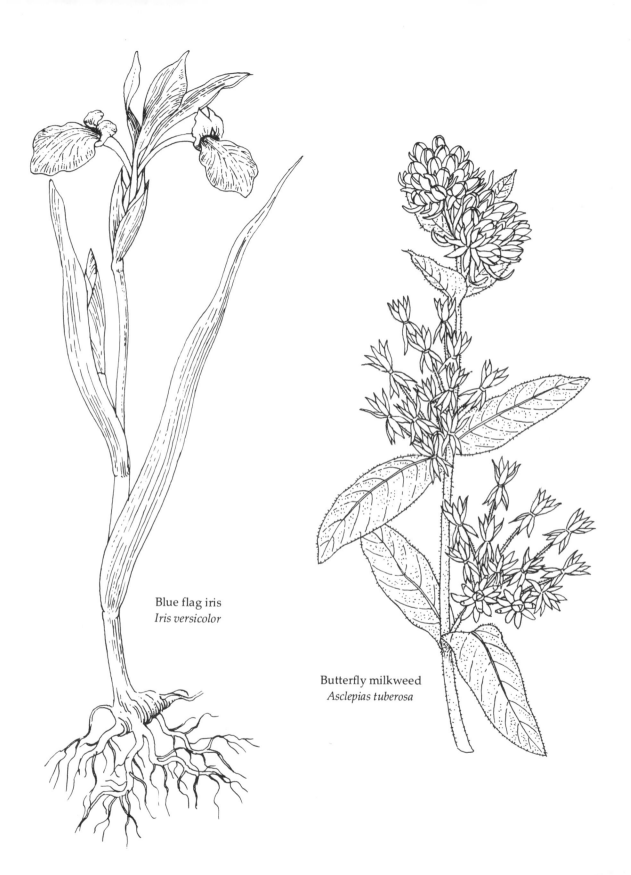

Blue flag iris
Iris versicolor

Butterfly milkweed
Asclepias tuberosa

Black-eyed Susan
Rudbeckia hirta

gryposepala, was a part of a recipe of several plants for urinary troubles, but the entire recipe has disappeared. The root of the columbine, *Aquilegia canadensis*, was enough by itself.

If one could not retain urine in his body, he was sometimes given a tea made from the entire plant of small skullcap, *Scutellaria parvula*.

Gravel in the urine, a very painful condition indeed, was treated by either of two groundsels, the golden groundsel, *Senecio aureus*, or the lamb's-tongue groundsel, *S. integerrimus*, though whether its virtues balanced its dangers is problematical. *Senecio* species can be poisonous.

Just general bladder trouble was soothed by a leaf tea made from entire-leaved rosinweed, *Silphium integrifolium*. Bladder trouble, which seems to be a broad general term, was also treated by the whole plant or root of the heart-leaved umbrellawort, *Mirabilis nyctaginea*; or the leaves and berries of the Virginia creeper, *Parthenocissus quinquefolia*, steeped in a medical dose.

If you have leaves of plantain, *Plantago major* and *P. rugeli*, steep them for urinary troubles; or make a leaf extract from bearberry, *Arctostaphylos uva-ursi*. Indians and explorers used the gray hairy leaves of the prairie sagewort, *Artemisia frigida*, as a diuretic.

Allegheny blackberry canes, *Rubus allegheniensis*, can be boiled for a diuretic tea, though it is a shame to destroy blackberry canes for a medicine when the berries are so delicious.

A stimulating kidney medicine was made by steeping the leaves of black-eyed Susan, *Rudbeckia hirta*. Like so many brightly colored flowers, the black-eyed Susan has accumulated many names, including yellow daisy, darkyhead, poorland daisy, golden Jerusalem, yellow oxeye daisy, English bull's-eye, brown daisy, brown Betty, and brown-eyed Susan.

Whites used several species of *Galium*, including the catchweed bedstraw or goose grass, *G. aparine*; shining bedstraw, *G. concinnum*; northern bedstraw, *G. boreale*; and fragrant or sweet-scented bedstraw, *G. triflorum*. The leaves of the thin-leaved sunflower, *Helianthus decapetalus*, were boiled.

We cannot miss finding the pretty blossoms of the oxeye daisy, *Chrysanthemum leucanthemum*, though the whole plant

140

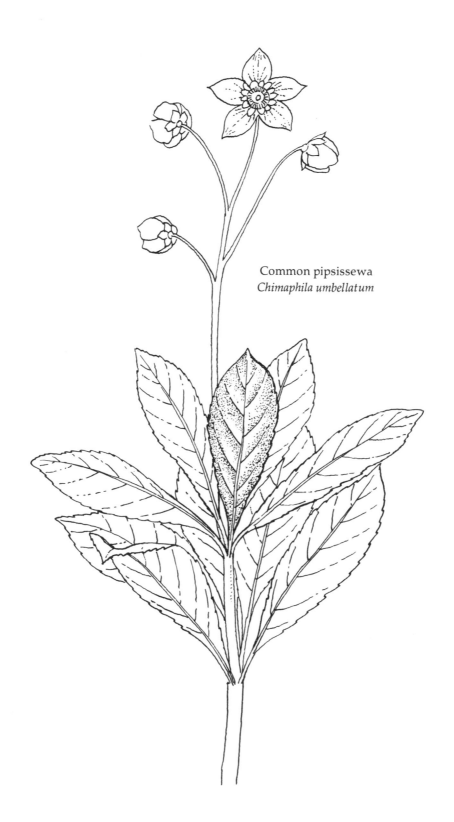

Common pipsissewa
Chimaphila umbellatum

141

Nannyberry
Viburnum lentago

Trumpet honeysuckle
Lonicera sempervirens

was dropped in the kettle to make the medical brew. At least three thistles were diuretics, including the Canada thistle, bull thistle, and field thistle, *Cirsium arvense, C. vulgare, C. discolor.* The little green shepherd's purse, *Capsella bursa-pastoris*, was believed to be valuable too.

Pipsissewa leaves provided a staple diuretic, a plant known as striped pipsissewa, spotted wintergreen, spotted pipsissewa, spotted piperidge, ratsbane, or dragon's-tongue, *Chimaphila maculata.* The common pipsissewa, *C. umbellatum*, was similar, though it had values not shared by the striped pipsissewa. Common pipsissewa was popularly called prince's pine, rheumatism weed, bitter wintergreen, ground holly, king's cure, love-in-winter, or pine tulip.

The scouring rush, *Equisetum hyemale*; the sylvan horsetail or wood horsetail, *E. sylvaticum*; and the field horsetail, *E. arvense*, were boiled to make a tea drunk for kidney troubles or dropsy. They all look rather much alike.

Butter-and-eggs or toadflax, *Linaria vulgaris*, was simmered for a tea made from the entire plant, beneficial particularly in dropsy.

Inflammations of the urinary passages sometimes yielded to a bark tea of slippery elm, *Ulmus rubra*, or the twigs of the white pine tree, *Pinus strobus*. Bark tea from either the blackhaw, *Viburnum prunifolium*, or the sweet viburnum, nannyberry, or sheepberry, *Viburnum lentago*, was brewed. Oriental cocklebur, *Xanthium orientale*; prickly ash, *Zanthoxylum americanum*; and the bark of the American fly honeysuckle, *Lonicera canadensis*, and all *Lonicera* species were diuretics.

If the urinary passages were inflamed, bark tea was drunk from the inner bark of eastern larch or tamarack, *Larix laricina*, at the same time inhaling dried powdered tamarack leaves.

A simpler medicine to increase the discharge of urine was made from the pink Philadelphia fleabane, *Erigeron philadelphicus*, in a steeped blossom decoction. Bladder trouble was treated by the unripe fruits of pear thorn, *Crataegus calpodendron*, cooked and eaten, or by a tea made from the twigs of the same tree.

Perhaps the most available medicine to increase the passage of urine was squash seeds pulverized, mixed with water and drunk. Squash and gourds of various sorts were raised by

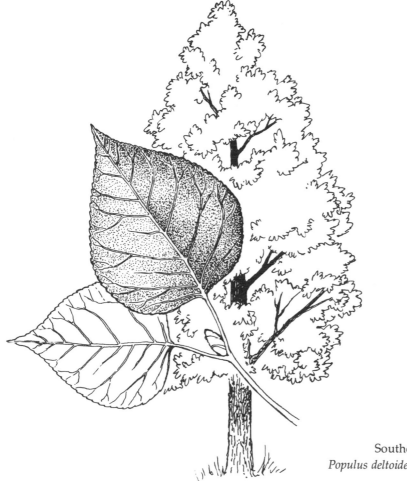

Southern poplar
Populus deltoides var. *missouriensis*

Indians since primitive times, and two whose seeds were
picked for this purpose were the pumpkin, *Cucurbita pepo*, and
the winter squash, *C. maxima*.

Bud resin from balm of Gilead, *X Populus gileadensis;* the
southern poplar, *Populus deltoides* var. *missouriensis;* and the
quaking aspen, *P. tremuloides*, made a kidney tonic. One
soaked the buds in alcohol, and took the dosage sparingly.

Slim nettles, *Urtica gracilis*, were known to have powerful
and peculiar diuretic properties, only for extreme cases.

A tea was made from hops, *Humulus* spp., which helped in
urinal troubles, still listed in United States pharmacopoeia for
such medication.

145

Juniper
Juniperus communis saxatilis
(photograph: Marjorie Morcom)

The pasqueflower, *Anemone patens*, delicate in its beauty though it may be, was another harvested for its diuretic properties even though the dried plants taken internally caused more trouble than cure. The dried rhizome and roots of elecampane, *Inula helenium*, was doubtless safer.

The white-tube star grass, *Aletris farinosa*, was not only classed as a medicine to help urinary discharge, it was also considered fine for other remedies as well. Pioneers found that corn silk from the fields of corn, *Zea mays*, would make as good a medicine to control urine discharge.

Bittersweet or woody nightshade, *Solanum dulcamara*, was known to be poisonous in both herbage and berries. Nevertheless the dried stems and branches were sometimes a diuretic to control the urine discharge. It had to be taken sparingly if at all.

In the deep woods, one could find the common juniper, *Juniperus communis*, hugging the ground. The ripe blue berries stimulated the flow of urine. Similarly the arborvitae, *Thuja occidentalis*, was searched for its dried leafy young twigs. Both of these are evergreens that could be found in the winter as well as the summer.

In South Dakota on the Sisseton Indian reservation, sweet flag, *Acorus calamus*, was combined with another root which remains a carefully guarded secret, the two boiled and drunk as a tea to take the place of insulin. It did not have good keeping qualities, and for that reason was made only in small amounts. Farther east in Wisconsin, whites found the small cranberry, *Vaccinium oxycoccos*, to make a tea which they believed to be beneficial against diabetes.

LIVER

The inner bark of either the butternut, *Juglans cinerea*, or the eastern black walnut, *J. nigra*, was said to be good for the liver. In the days of self-medication one often referred to an undefined ailment as liver trouble, not knowing exactly where the seat of the illness was. Besides, it sounded much more important than "feeling poorly" if one could say plaintively, "I'm feeling liverish." If one felt liverish he took something that was

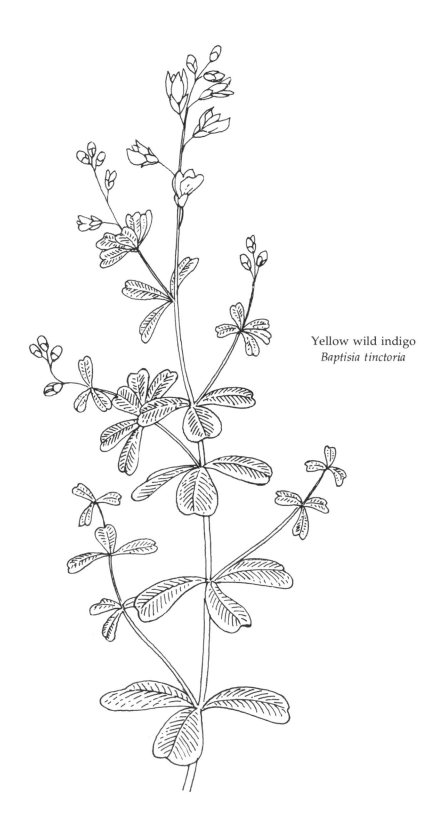

Yellow wild indigo
Baptisia tinctoria

147

good for the liver, naturally. Of course the phrase did have the colloquial meaning (if describing somebody else) of being crabby or cross. "He's feeling liverish" could mean simply "I just can't live with him today, he's so ornery."

The stem bark of the eastern wahoo, *Euonymus atropurpurea*, was taken in small quantities as a liver stimulant; or you could boil the root of blue flag, *Iris versicolor*. A root tea made from self-heal or heal-all, *Prunella vulgaris*, was not only good for the liver but was a general tonic as well.

Leaves of bracken, *Pteridium aquilinum*, boiled with sugar were also believed to be a liver tonic, though it is known now that bracken leaves if eaten by cattle make them so sick that they just don't care, in fact too sick to live. It seems in the light of this knowledge that we might prefer to feel liverish rather than drink bracken leaf tea.

The sharp-lobed hepatica, *Hepatica acutiloba*, was popularly known as liverleaf. The pale-blue hepatica had leaves shaped like liver lobes, hence it was believed to cure liver disorders. The yellow wild indigo, *Baptisia tinctoria*, had no such shape to commend it but the dried roots stimulated the liver. Oregon grape or other *Mahonia* species were pulled for their roots as a liver medication.

Even old pharmacy handbooks listed some of these plants. The common mayapple or mandrake, *Podophyllum peltatum*, was so listed, as was Culver's physic, *Veronicastrum virginicum*. The dried rhizome and roots were suggested as the medication.

LUNGS

When one thinks of lung trouble and wild plants in the same moment, the logical plant to connect the two is pleurisy root or butterfly weed, *Asclepias tuberosa*. This brightest of all milkweeds is still familiarly called pleurisy root, and its small clustered flowers are brilliant orange yellow in meadows and fields. Other names for it include Canada root, Indian posy, orangeroot, orange swallowwort, tuber root, whiteroot, windroot, and yellow or orange milkweed. It is found prolifically in the eastern half of the United States and Canada, though

Sunflower
Helianthus annuus

one can find it in parts of the West. The method of treatment
for pleurisy is not complicated. One digs the plant, washes the
root, and chews the root as it is, raw and unencumbered by
boiling water.

Other plants known for their ability to help lung diseases
need boiling to make a liquid medicine. One of the sunflowers,
Helianthus annuus, is still known by reservation Indians in the
Dakotas as a remedy for pulmonary ailments. They boil sunflower heads and drink the medicine. A sunflower found in
eastern areas for the lungs was the woodland sunflower,
Helianthus strumosus, but its root was simmered rather than the
blossom.

149

Maidenhair fern
Adiantum modestum

Another lung infusion is made from the tops and leaves of the sticky-head, *Grindelia squarrosa*. Also called curlycup or gumweed, it is common on dry plains.

If you have a pain in the lungs or have difficulty breathing because of a cold or other respiratory ailment, you can prepare bastard toadflax, *Comandra umbellata*, in either of two ways. Make a leaf tea and drink; or if there are immature flowers on the plant you can lick them as you would a modern lozenge or cough drop.

The common burdock, *Arctium minus*, or great burdock, *A. lappa*, might be a weed to many, but there have been those who searched for its small lavender florets and broad leaves. They wanted the root, which they believed would help pleurisy.

The inner bark of white pine, *Pinus strobus*, was steeped to cure a pain in the chest, an old practice among Indians that was copied by settlers when they boiled white pine bark as a basis for cough syrup. The bark of the black oak, *Quercus velutina*, or red oak, *Q. rubra*, was also cooked for the lungs. The inner bark of the balsam fir, *Abies balsamea*, was steeped for chest pains, and the balsam gum itself was an external medication in lung trouble.

Root tea made from bog valerian, *Valeriana uliginosa*, had a feeble sedative in it for soothing lungs. For a simple pain in the chest, drink root tea made from dandelion, *Taraxacum officinale*; or try steeping the flowers of flat-topped goldenrod, *Solidago graminifolia*.

When they were not sure, but hurt in the chest and suspected lung trouble, groundsel tea was taken. Golden groundsel, *Senecio aureus*, and lamb's-tongue groundsel, *S. integerrimus*, were both found, the first is also called golden ragwort and the second entire-leaved groundsel. These are no longer recommended, being known to be toxic.

The leaves of bracken, *Pteridium aquilinum*, were boiled with sugar to make a soothing syrup for general lung trouble. The root of the carrion flower or greenbrier, *Smilax herbacea*, combatted general lung troubles; and the bark of the American plane tree or sycamore, *Platanus occidentalis*, may be eaten for vague hurting just as it comes from the tree.

If one had a chronic affection of the respiratory tract, he

Canada hemlock
Tsuga canadensis

could make a syrup or infusion of maidenhair fern, *Adiantum pedatum*, a mixture that controlled a cough as well as lung pains.

Root tea from yellow taenidia or yellow pimpernel, *Taenidia integerrima*, was drunk for lung troubles, then after the root had been steeped for the tea the rest of the goodness was saved by chewing the boiled root.

An easy remedy for lung trouble was that made by boiling twigs of the American linden, *Tilia americana*. Some folks believed in poultices, and thought bronchitis and pleurisy might be helped by slapping a plaster on the chest made from bark and pitch of the eastern hemlock, *Tsuga canadensis*, but one finds more tea remedies for the lungs than plasters.

Generally speaking, lung diseases were treated by dried violet plants of almost any species, but the Canada violet, *Viola canadensis*, and the American dog violet, *V. conspersa*, were considered best.

Scurvy pea
Psoralea tenuiflora

Violet
Viola canadensis

Virginia bluebells
Mertensia virginica

Ripe berries of prickly ash, *Zanthoxylum americanum*, were cooked in hot water, and the liquid sprayed on chest or throat for bronchial diseases or sores. The liquid could be drunk for added protection, and if you added some bark to the brew mixture it was thought to lessen coughs and the hemorrhages of tuberculosis.

Though the berries, root, flowers, and leaves of jimsonweed, *Datura stramonium*, are acknowledged to be poisonous, the leaves were said to be an asthma remedy at one time, rolled and smoked like cigarettes. The plant has pure white handsome flowers, but a very disagreeable smell and a worse reaction. It is best to leave this one alone.

Asthma was also treated by frontiersmen by boiling the dried bark of the highbush cranberry, *Viburnum opulus*, then drinking it. Asthma is a rough illness, and we do not wonder that they searched for some kind of a remedy. The little Virginia bluebells nodding on their slender stems were also said to cure chest illnesses. One of the names for this plant was smooth lungwort, *Mertensia virginica*, which obviously came from the old belief connected with it.

A tea from the dried leaves and flowering tops of the white horseweed or butterweed, *Erigeron canadensis*, treated bronchitis by clearing the accumulated mucus.

For almost any of the ailments touching the lungs, tea was made from dye bedstraw, *Galium tinctorium*, thought to be good for clearing mucus, asthma, cough, or chronic bronchitis. The dye bedstraw is often called small cleavers, stiff marsh bedstraw, or wild madder. Another was made from the roots of *Heliopsis scabra*, rough oxeye or false sunflower.

Root of the great St.-John's-wort, *Hypericum ascyron*, was mixed with other roots to treat weak lungs or consumption in Indian tribes, though whites used the fresh root drug alone for chronic catarrhal conditions of the lungs and a leaf concoction to loosen mucous accumulations in the throat caused by catarrh or colds. Those mixed with it included the berries of the staghorn sumac, *Rhus typhina*; and the root of the western red raspberry, *Rubus idaeus* var. *aculeatissimus*.

Root tea from blue flag, *Iris versicolor*, treated lung troubles from colds to deep-seated chest symptoms. If you have pneumonia for sure, you need a hot mixed infusion of Canada

Purple-stem angelica
Angelica atropurpurea

or American mint, *Mentha arvensis* var.; catnip, *Nepeta cataria;* and peppermint, *Mentha piperita*. Drink some of the hot brew, and saturate a poultice with the rest of it to lay on your chest. If you like mint, the smell must be heavenly in such a concentrated treatment.

The root of the hop tree, *Ptelea trifoliata*, called three-leaved hop tree, was combined with three other barks, pounded, and steeped for tea, or a warm root infusion of purple-stem angelica, *Angelica atropurpurea*, was known.

One more gave its root for bronchial troubles such as consumption or tuberculosis, *Psoralea tenuiflora*, called slim-flowered scurf pea, scurvy pea, or few-flowered psoralea and found on plains or foothills. One must find the roots of two other plants whose identities have been lost, and boil the three together.

155

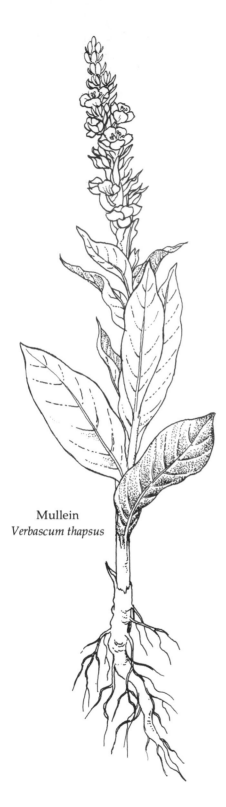

Mullein
Verbascum thapsus

We do have one complete recipe for you. Pick the leaves of the flannel mullein, *Verbascum thapsus*, before blooming time, combine with the leaves of the butterbur or coltsfoot, *Petasites palmata*, which have been dried powdery fine in a small fire. Add root of plum, *Prunus americana*, and glycerine to make a syrup which was probably taken in the manner of cough syrup. You will recognize the mullein easily. Its erect height of several feet and woolly leaves are topped by a spike of yellow flowers. The coltsfoot will be more difficult unless you live in a location favorable to its growth. In some areas it is called sweet coltsfoot, palmate-leaf sweet coltsfoot, or just butterbur. Actually the mullein was prepared in several ways for lung troubles. The root was boiled and drunk. The leaves were smoked alone to relieve asthma and bronchitis. The fully opened flowers were steeped for tuberculosis. Common names included quite a list—great mullein, mullein dock, velvet dock, Aaron's rod, Adam's flannel, old-man's-flannel, blanket leaf, bullock's lungwort, cow's lungwort, clown's lungwort, candlewick, feltwort, flannelleaf, hare's-beard, and velvet plant.

Nobody ever cured tuberculosis with herbs, but it was said that the root of bittersweet, *Celastrus scandens*, made a medicine that would alleviate the symptoms. In fact, the mullein-coltsfoot-plum root recipe just quoted was sometimes altered to include bittersweet root instead of mullein root. Some thought the butterbur roots were enough alone to heal bronchial and lung troubles, either boiled to make a medicinal beverage or dried and smoked in a pipe as people once did in Germany and Sweden.

The root of either the black cherry, *Prunus serotina*, or the chokecherry, *Prunus virginiana*, made a medical tea to combat tuberculosis. The root of the American water lily, *Nymphaea odorata*, made a cough medicine believed to be of particular value in tuberculosis treatment, and it was said that the drug sweet flag or calamus, *Acorus calamus*, had the same qualities.

Others were root tea from candle anemone, *Anemone cylindrica*, and from rattlesnake fern, *Botrychium virginianum*, called Virginia grape fern or hemlock-leaved moonwort.

A dried blossom tea was made from blueberry elder, *Sambucus caerulea*, to combat consumption or any bleeding from the lungs; and some tribes used the potentially dangerous root

American water lily
Nymphaea odorata

bark of the American elder, *Sambucus canadensis*, for a medicine
to free the lungs of phlegm.

The leaves of the blue American bellflower, *Campanula
americana*, called tall bellflower, made a tea as a lung remedy
for coughs or consumption, but a related flower as delicately
blue was the bluebell known as harebell, *Campanula
rotundifolia*, of which the root was needed and combined with
other plants for lung troubles. Some people know the harebell

157

Tall bellflower
Campanula americana

Harebell
Campanula rotundifolia

as bluebells-of-Scotland, thimbles, lady's thimble, heath bells, witches' bells, or round-leaved bellflower. Usually the round basal leaf which identifies with its name is gone by the time the blossoms appear.

A root tea for consumption was made from gray dogwood, *Cornus racemosa*. Settlers found the weed called hound's-tongue or beggar's-lice, *Cynoglossum officinale*, to treat bronchial and pulmonary affections, though it is questionable now whether they made a tea or a smoke inhalant.

CHILDBIRTH AND CHILD CARE

CHILDBIRTH

The year was sometime in the nineteenth century, maybe earlier, a time before the white men moved onto the Western prairies. In the Indian village two women looked sadly at the puny infant in his mother's arms.

"He is so little," said one.

"Will he live, do you think?" asked the other.

His mother cuddled the child closely. "Find some joe-pye weed for me," she said. "We'll bathe him in it as often as we can. That will strengthen him. He will grow."

The joe-pye weed, *Eupatorium purpureum*, is a flowering plant that likes to grow along streams, its flat-topped blossoms a pinkish bundle of beauty in season. The Indian women boiled the roots for the medical bath that was believed to strengthen a baby. If it did not have immediate results, the mother bathed the child until it was sometimes six years old before giving up the joe-pye weed baths.

There are many references to the difficulties of childbirth in old stories and handbooks, indicating that babies have been problems in birthing for Indian mothers as well as among the civilized whites. As time passed it became apparent that some of the plants used by the Indians had curative powers that

159

have since been adapted to modern medicines. Joe-pye weed
was gathered by white settlers as a stimulant among other
reasons, though whether its stimulant properties would have
been beneficial in bathing an infant is another question. But
there were many plants, and many needs.

If you are the saddest of females, a woman who wants a
baby and does not conceive, you might try the old folklore
drink made from the bark of common ninebark, *Physocarpus
opulifolius*, once believed to encourage fertility. Having become
pregnant, the root of the wild sarsaparilla, *Aralia nudicaulis*,
was one of the first plants they searched. Pounded and boiled
as a tea, it was drunk as a blood purifier during pregnancy.
Even in this century, the wild sarsaparilla is gathered for its
crude drug properties, mainly as a stimulant.

The root of blue cohosh, *Caulophyllum thalictroides*, was
boiled for a tea to prevent abortion, to suppress profuse menstruation, and for uterine diseases, though it was generally
confined to primitive Indian tribes and rarely used by whites.
The blue cohosh was also known as papooseroot, squawroot,
blueberry root, blue ginseng, and yellow ginseng, the first two
names referring to its childbirth properties. This is another
recognized today for its medicinal properties primarily in
genitourinary remedies.

To stop vomiting in pregnancy, one could drink tea made
from the cup rosinweed, *Silphium perfoliatum*, popularly known
as cup plant, square-stem, angle stem, rosinweed, Indian cup,
or ragged cup. Indian women also took it to reduce profuse
menstruation, and white women contended that all *Silphium*
species had that quality. Though the *Silphium* species are not
listed as a popular drug plant gathered today, they were used
by white settlers for a variety of remedies not necessarily
connected with pregnancy.

During pregnancy the tiny Canada mayflower, *Maianthemum
canadense*, was found to keep the kidneys open. Called false lily
of the valley, wild lily of the valley, cowslip, bead-ruby, one
leaf, and one blade, this white blossom hides from the casual
observer for the delight of the sharper-eyed sleuths.

It was believed that if a woman drank a tea made from the
leaves and flowers of the hardhack spiraea or steeplebush,
Spiraea tomentosa, she would not only avoid pregnancy sickness

Sweet fern
Comptonia peregrina

but would also have an easier time giving birth to her baby. Frontier settlers boiled the root and leaves of the plant to combat diseased genitourinary tracts, and called the plant silverleaf, silverweed, whitecap, meadowsweet, poor man's soap, spice hardhack, or rosy bush.

Yellow beadlily or northern clintonia, *Clintonia borealis*, could be made into a tea that if drunk by an expectant mother would help in the physical birth of the baby. Lacking that, sweet fern, *Comptonia peregrina*, could be tried. The entire sweet fern plant

161

was steeped, especially the leaves and tops, as they are gathered even today for a variety of medications.

Slippery elm root tea was also believed to make childbirth easier. The slippery elm, *Ulmus fulva*, has a mucilaginous quality that would certainly suggest a baby sliding from its mother's womb with ease, and that may have been why that idea originated. This is another that has kept its medicinal qualities into the twentieth century, and is known for healing in several ways.

Root fibers of the glade mallow, *Napaea dioica*, were boiled to make the birthing easier, too, though I found no indication that it is still used in that way. In primitive days on the prairies young mothers kept the glade mallow root handy in case trouble developed in the female organs after the baby was born.

When childbirth was imminent, an expectant mother drank a root tea made from pitcher plant, *Sarracenia purpurea*, a brew recognized as a mild tonic, laxative and diuretic as well.

For mothers actually in labor, the root of the smaller burdock, *Arctium minus*, was steeped with the root of bittersweet, *Celastrus scandens*, and an umbelliferous root. To give them strength, they were administered root tea made from Culver's physic, *Veronicastrum virginicum*. The burdock root and bittersweet are part of today's medications, and it appears that its efficacy in childbirth was mainly because of its emetic properties. The Culver's physic is a strong physic sometimes referred to as Leptandra in drug catalogs.

For relieving the pain of childbirth, a brew was made from the root of the wild yam, *Dioscorea villosa*. The yam tea had other medical properties, some of which were indicated in its popular names, colicroot, rheumatism root, devil's-bones. Though its rootstock is still gathered today, it is not certain whether it is still wanted for childbirth or not.

A root tea was made from red baneberry, *Actaea rubra*, and white baneberry, *A. pachypoda*, to relieve the pain of childbirth, and was accepted by either whites or Indian women as a remedy for uterine pains. The white baneberry had its share of popular names, including white cohosh, white beads, necklaceweed, whiteberry, and snakeroot. The *Actaea* berries are poisonous, and even the rootstock is known today to be a

Prickly lettuce
Lactuca serriola

Blue lettuce
Lactuca biennis

violent purgative, irritant and emetic, so the root tea administered in frontier times must have been taken in very small quantities to be of any value.

If a young mother went into convulsions while giving birth to her child, she was given a tea of dried bark from the highbush cranberry, *Viburnum opulus*, to stop the convulsions and aid with the childbirth. The cranberry bush bark is recognized by today's pharmacists as an antispasmodic or cramp remedy.

After childbirth, a young mother could hasten the flow of milk from her breasts by drinking a leaf tea made from either prickly lettuce, *Lactuca serriola*, or blue lettuce, *L. biennis*, some-

163

times called milkweed. The prickly lettuce could be saved to make a medical syrup for babies' diseases. Sometimes called just wild lettuce, the prickly lettuce was often known as wild opium, a bright-green plant two to seven feet high covered with a whitish bloom. Pharmacists have indicated that *Lactuca* dried milk juice is a sedative; perhaps it helped to relax a mother enough so her milk could flow easier.

For caked breasts, they dried the root of the sensitive fern, *Onoclea sensibilis*, powdered it, and made a tea for the mother to drink. It was said that root tea made from bracken, *Pteridium aquilinum*, could soften caked breasts, too, although bracken fronds can be dangerous. The root of the Andrews or closed gentian, *Gentiana andrewsi*, was another searched for caked breasts, though in this case the root itself was eaten. White settlers ate the Andrews gentian root just to promote the appetite.

Pains in the breast after childbirth were said to lessen after drinking a root tea made from lady fern, *Athyrium filix-femina*.

After childbirth twig tea from frost grape, *Vitis vulpina*, was drunk; the brew was popular among both whites and Indians for many reasons including the fact that it just tasted good. A root tea was also made from the long-style sweetroot or smooth sweet cicely, *Osmorhiza longistylis*, which a new mother drank for her general health when she gave birth to a child. The tea had a distinctly licorice flavor, not at all bad-tasting. The smooth sweet cicely looks a lot like poison hemlock, so one must be extremely careful in gathering the plant.

Prairie allionia or wild four-o'clock, *Mirabilis nyctaginea*, was the medicine for abdominal swelling after childbirth. It had other values too, as did many of the plants, but if a mother felt that she did not return to normalcy as she should after the birth of her baby she could drink a decoction of the root of the prairie allionia known popularly as wild four-o'clock, umbrellawort, or heart-leaved umbrellawort. Look for it along streams and waste places. It grows two to three feet high; its leaves are opposite each other and its small flowers are a pretty red to top the tall stem.

To clear up afterbirth, a root tea was made from snowberry, *Symphoricarpos albus*, a cultivated plant called waxberry, snowdrop berry, or egg plant; or from the western snowberry called

164

Snowberry
Symphoricarpos albus

wolfberry, buckbrush, or buckbush, *S. occidentalis*. This medication does not appear to have lasted through the centuries, as one finds little reference to it now.

To clear the system after the birth of the baby, the mother drank tea from boiling the stems of scouring rush, *Equisetum hyemale*, a medication which apparently acted as an intestinal and urethral astringent.

The tiny cones of low birch, *Betula pumila*, were steeped for a tea which new mothers drank after childbirth, and later during difficult menstrual periods.

If a baby was born dead and the mother lay in pain after a difficult childbirth ordeal, she was sometimes given a dose of bark tea made from the common elder, *Sambucus canadensis*.

165

Since the bark tea was also known to be a strong intestinal
purge, one wonders what was accomplished by subjecting the
mother to additional misery—but perhaps it helped.

If a mother tended to hemorrhage with childbirth, she was
given a tea from the whole plant of the smaller pussytoes,
Antennaria neodioca, smaller or lesser cat's-foot, that soft-
flowered little plant that could be rather inconspicuous if one
did not look for it. The leaves of the plantain-leaved pussytoes,
A. plantaginifolia, made as good an after-childbirth tea if you
could not find the smaller pussytoes. The plantain-leafed pussytoes is called plantain-leaved everlasting, pussytoes, cat's-
foot, cat's-paws or everlasting.

Uterine hemorrhages and menstrual troubles were also treated
by a medical tea made of the leaves of bearberry, *Arctostaphylos
uva-ursi*. The bearberry leaves have an astringent property that
has been recognized even in the twentieth century.

The berries of smooth sumac, *Rhus glabra*, could be boiled to
stop hemorrhage in women. A root bark tea of the same shrub
would also stop the bleeding. The staghorn sumac, *R. typhina*,
being much more hairy than the smooth sumac in the tops or
twigs of the shrub, was considered therefore to be better suited
to diseases of the hairy female. These plants were known in an
era when chemical analysis was out of the question, so reasons
for using them could be very simple and naive; nevertheless
smooth sumac leaves, bark, and berries are still gathered for
their recognized medicinal value in some areas, and pharmaceutical books recognize the sumac berries as a refrigerant
and astringent.

If with the birth of a baby the womb had been injured, it
could be healed with a root tea mixture in which bigroot lady's
thumb or swamp persicaria, *Polygonum coccineum*, was included. The Pennsylvania persicaria, Pennsylvania smartweed,
P. pensylvanicum, could be substituted for or with the swamp
persicaria.

If a mother had so many children that she began to have
uterine trouble, she could try a root tea from prickly
gooseberry, *Ribes cynosbati*. Another uterine tonic was made
from the dried rhizome and roots of the white-tube star grass,
Aletris farinosa; but if one wanted a sedative for that organ the
white population of pioneer days made a brew from the

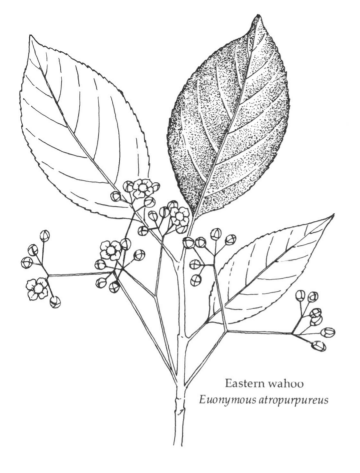

Eastern wahoo
Euonymous atropurpureus

mountain maple, *Acer spicatum*. For uterine trouble of un-specified character, a decoction from the inner bark of eastern wahoo, *Euonymus atropurpurea*, was thought to be helpful. This little tree does not extend far west but its bright-red fruit can be found on the eastern edge of the plains up and down the United States. It is known by many names: burning brush or burning bush, spindle tree, Indian arrowwood, bursting heart, strawberry tree, strawberry bush, American spindle tree, bitter ash, and pegwood.

Of this group, Remington's 1917 pharmaceutical book notes that the *Aletris farinosa* dried rhizome and roots were a uterine tonic then, and that the wahoo dried root bark could be used with caution but was uncertain and irregular in its effects.

Puffballs, *Lycoperdon* spp., made a styptic for the umbilicus

167

of the newborn infant. It is listed under the name of Lycoperdon spores in pharmacopoeias as a hemostatic and surgical dusting powder, so definitely the old folklore was on the right track there. When possible, the newborn baby was also washed with liquid from boiled reindeer moss, *Cladonia rangiferina*, a moss which was found on old tree stumps.

Very young babies when sick were sometimes bathed in a solution from the leaves of Texas croton or skunkweed, *Croton texensis*, but it must have been a weak infusion because croton oil can be very irritating to the skin.

On the other hand, when a child was late in learning to talk or laugh, the Meskwaki Indians of Wisconsin believed that if he were bathed in a broth made by cooking the bone of an animal that had died when the child was born, with some Canada goldenrod, *Solidago canadensis*, the magic combination would help the child. We can understand the goldenrod very well, but we are puzzled now in this twentieth century as to how they found an animal that died when the child was born, at the late date of when the same child should be talking. Did they save a bone, in case?

FEMALE MALADIES

Between pregnancies, white and Indian women of our frontiers knew many plants that helped in their general health.

Two groundsels were female regulators, both called squaw-weed in that connection. One was the golden groundsel or golden ragwort, *Senecio aureus*, called liferoot, swamp squawweed, grundy-swallow, or false valerian. The other was the lamb's-tongue groundsel, *Senecio integerrimus*, or entire-leaved groundsel. Both can be dangerous.

The leaves of tansy, *Tanacetum vulgare*, were brewed to promote natural menstruation when needed; or they sometimes tried a tea made from prickly ash, *Zanthoxylum americanum*.

The leaf of the Canada sagebrush, *Artemisia canadensis*, and angelica root were combined for menstruation troubles of more indefinite nature; though the leaves of St. Louis sagebrush, *A. ludoviciana*, were brewed alone in a tea for genital troubles.

Prickly ash
Zanthoxylum americanum

If menstruation ceased because of a cold, one drank a tea
steeped from the dried inner bark of the eastern arborvitae,
Thuja occidentalis.

For irregularity of the menses, women drank the stimulating
tea made from the steeped grated root of large-flowered trillium or wake-robin, *Trillium grandiflorum*. Once called birthroot, it was also taken to make the birthing of a baby easier. *T.
erectum* was called birthroot too, as well as purple trillium or
beth root, partly from its promotion of the menstrual discharge
in women who were having trouble.

The purple-stem angelica, *Angelica atropurpurea*, was known
to be as good a medicine for the purpose, and if a woman
could not find the angelica she could sometimes find a
marigold, *Calendula officinalis*, the dried florets of which would
do as well besides calming the cramps that might accompany
menstruation. Another that was raised in pioneer gardens as

169

well as our modern gardens was the thyme, *Thymus vulgaris*. Thyme tops were collected when the plant was in flower, dried, and saved to control menstruation and cramps.

Profuse menstruation was treated by a root tea made from white verbena, *Verbena urticaefolia*.

A tea was made of the small green shepherd's purse, *Capsella bursa-pastoris*, to promote menstruation when needed. Shepherd's purse has quaint little heart-shaped pods, and boasts a variety of names—shepherd's bag, shepherd's pouch, St. James' weed, caseweed, mother's-heart, pickpurse, pickpocket, lady's-purse, witches' pouches, shovelweed, pepper plant, and toywort, Bogbean or buckbean, *Menyanthes trifoliata*, would do the same if taken in small quantities, but tea from catnip, *Nepeta cataria*, was safer and accomplished the same thing.

Female maladies, speaking broadly, were treated by a mixture of the blades, stem, and root of maidenhair fern, *Adiantum pedatum*, though we are not sure how it was prepared. Maidenhair fern root mixed with the root of sharp-lobed hepatica or liverleaf, *Hepatica acutiloba*, was said to cure vaginal discharges such as leucorrhea. Some knew the hepatica as sharp-lobed liverleaf, heart liverleaf, liverwort, or mayflower.

Yarrow leaves of either the common yarrow, *Achillea millefolium*, or woolly yarrow, *A. lanulosa*, were gathered for various ailments of the reproductive organs. Perhaps the tannic content of the white oak, *Quercus alba*, or the bur oak, *Q. macrocarpa*, was the valuable agent when one boiled the inner bark for an infusion to counteract vaginal inflammations or infections. The American water lily called sweet white water lily, *Nymphaea odorata*, treated undetermined inflammations; though leucorrhea was best dosed by the root of the yellow pond lily, *Nuphar advena*. Other general women's medicines were made from the fruit and bark of the hawthorn tree, *Crataegus* spp.; or from the leaves of the American red currant, *Ribes triste*.

For vague female ills, the stems of pumpkin, *Cucurbita pepo*, were ground and boiled as a beneficial tea. The largeleaf avens, *Geum macrophyllum*, was a female remedy of tonic and astringent properties, as was a root tea made from dotted gayfeather, *Liatris punctata*.

Common self-heal
Prunella vulgaris

171

The root of the wild parsnip called garden parsnip, *Pastinaca sativa*, is said to be poisonous in its wild state when in bloom, though cultivation has made it a most desirable vegetable. Wild, it was a cautious medicine, a minute quantity being mixed with four other roots to make a tea for female troubles. Popular names included madnep, tank, queen weed, birds' nest, and hart's-eye.

White rattlesnake root, called white lettuce, *Prenanthes alba*, was searched to combat female diseases either in a decoction of the leaves or the root.

The root of the self-heal or heal-all, *Prunella vulgaris*, was mixed with others to act as a female remedy.

Bunchberry
Cornus canadensis

SPECIAL CHILDREN'S MEDICINES

A root tea mild enough for treating colic in babies was made from the root of the low-growing bunchberry, *Cornus canadensis*, that clean little shrub of the woods that hugs the ground. Colic could be treated by boiled ginseng root, too. Chop the boiled ginseng, *Panax quinquefolium*, and feed it to the baby. Of the many colic remedies listed for the family, the bunchberry tea and ginseng root are the only ones we found particularly designated for babies.

The heart-leaved umbrellawort or wild four-o'clock, *Mirabilis nyctaginea*, valued for abdominal swelling after childbirth, was also indicated for healing a sore mouth in babies. The directions tell us to grind the dried root fine, and that is as far as we are instructed. Babies being individualists at best, we hope the dried root tasted delicious if they wanted the little ones to accept a spoonful in their mouths. Not having tried it, we really have no right to comment.

Another mouthwash so gentle that it was given to babies suffering from sore throats or teething soreness was that made from the roots of goldthread, *Coptis groenlandica*. In spite of its gentle action, it was said to have curative powers even against cankers in the mouth.

As we have milder medicines for our children than we have for adults, so we read that "the bark of the root of any species

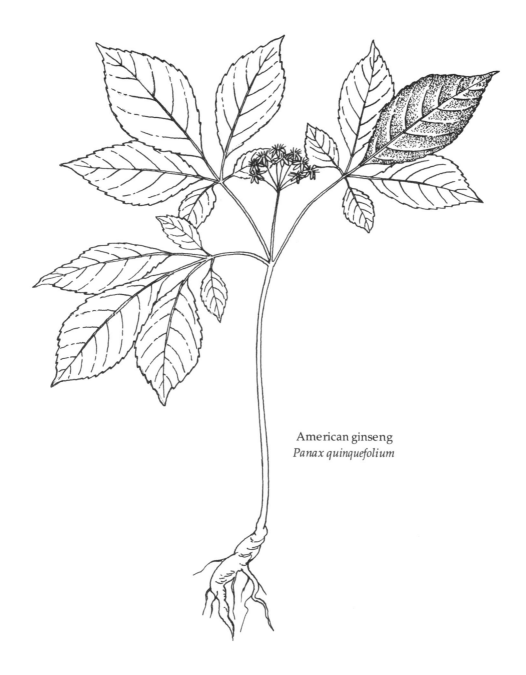

American ginseng
Panax quinquefolium

173

Box elder
Acer negundo

Virginia strawberry
Fragaria virginiana

of oak was scraped off, and boiled and the decoction given for bowel trouble, especially in children."[1]

Particular emphasis is given to the bark of the bur oak, *Quercus macrocarpa*, and the red oak, *Q. rubra*, both of which grow over the midwest. Their irregularly shaped leaves are recognized by anyone. No other leaf is like the oak leaf, and no other nut is like its acorn.

If a child was constipated, there were laxatives. Two which are still remembered are the teas made of the fresh inner bark of slippery elm or red elm tree, *Ulmus rubra*; or the inner bark of the box elder tree, *Acer negundo*. Like the oak, a bark tea

[1]Melvin R. Gilmore, *Uses of Plants by the Indians of the Missouri River Region.* Bureau of American Ethnology report 1911–1912. Washington, D.C.: Government Printing Office, 1919. p. 75.

was made from bitternut hickory, *Carya cordiformis*, for simple stomach trouble, making the bowels loose in minor constipation.

A root tea especially for stomach ache in babies or for bowel trouble in children was made from the Virginia strawberry, *Fragaria virginiana*, or scarlet strawberry. If one of the children was nauseated, it was a simple matter to find some ragweed, *Ambrosia elatior*, and make a dressing of the bruised leaves to lay on a small scarified abdomen. It must have worked at times, because it is listed as an accepted practice. Ragweed is common. It should not have been hard to find. Look for a tall coarse stalk with hairy stems, topped by spikes of small seed-like flowers. Along dusty highways the entire plant may appear grayish, but it is so scattered that it has acquired many names—Roman wormwood, hogweed, bitterweed, stickweed, stammerwort, blackweed or tassel weed, and hay-fever weed.

Whopping cough is very much a children's disease, and for the relief of the cough our grandmothers collected the leaves of the chestnut tree, *Castanea dentata*, in September or October before they turned color, dried them, and made a respiratory sedative said to be effective.

If the child had only a cold, it was simpler to treat it with onion juice. One way of making onion cold medicine was to wrap the onion in a wet rag, toss it in the ashes to cook, strain it, and mix it with sugar. The onion syrup was said to cure a cold, but if not it would at least help the child to go to sleep. Some parents prepared the syrup to combat even an attack of the hives in children.

Various home remedies for colds were made from onions, and told to us by our own grandmothers. Pioneer women knew them well, and could have found the wild onions, *Allium* spp., as well as the big Bermuda onions available today. Another recipe was to put a big pan of sliced onions (a peck is about right) under the bed of the child who has the cold. The fumes do the trick. We distinctly remember drinking another onion syrup for colds, too, teaspoonful by teaspoonful as we needed it, and licking the spoon for every drop. Our onion syrup was made by interlacing sliced onions and sugar to a syrup stage, and we loved it. This was a simple remedy, but if it soothed a raw throat, who can say it was useless?

FEVER

Fever hits anybody, any age, any time. This discussion of plants used for fever would apply to adults as well as children, but we include it with children's problems because a child develops a fever so easily and so often that it seems the most familiar problem a worried mother has to face. Doubtless most of the fever remedies were given sparingly for children, in stronger doses for adults. Some were for specifically children's diseases such as measles.

Most medicines for fever were decoctions of root, fruits, or leaves, depending on the plant, and taken internally in prescribed doses. Our friends the calamus root, *Acorus calamus*, and the wild licorice, *Glycyrrhiza lepidota*, belong to this group. Boil the root of the calamus root, and of the wild or American licorice.

The prairie allionia or wild four-o'clock, *Mirabilis nyctaginea*, blue cohosh, *Caulophyllum thalictroides*, and little rattlepod, *Astragalus caroliniana*, must all be dug for their roots to make fever medicine. Boil the wild four-o'clock root and drink the concoction. The blue cohosh, named perhaps for its pair of blue berrylike seeds rather than for its inconspicuous bronzy-green flowers, has a thick running stem as an underground system. This root is said to be most effective when boiled. The blue cohosh needs rich woodland soil. Look for it where the trees grow, but leave it there. It is rare!

Golden zizia root was wanted for fevers, a plant also known as golden Alexander, early or golden meadow parsnip, or wild parsley, *Zizia aurea*. Purple tall meadowrue, *Thalictrum dasycarpum*, provided a root tea that reduced fever, too.

The little rattlepod is one of the loco weeds, and its root decoction was specified for fever in children, so one may assume that it was considered less potent than some of the other fever remedies. Search for small yellowish-green flowers on a long cluster topping a tall stalk.

Dried leaves collected from the older parts of the eucalyptus tree, *Eucalyptus globulus*, were said to be good for a fever; and the little creeping hollygrape, *Mahonia repens*, so like the Oregon grape, was pulled for its rhizome and roots for the same reason. If you limit yourself to small quantities only, it is

Little rattlepod
Astragalus canadensis var. *carolinianus*

177

said that the yellow wild indigo, *Baptisia tinctoria*, could yield a fever medicine from its dried roots.

You could try a root tea for the ague made from the Indian hemp or dogbane, *Apocynum cannabinum*; the shining bedstraw, *Galium concinnum*; or the catchweed bedstraw, *G. aparine*, called goose grass. The white-tube star grass, *Aletris farinosa*, was known in one day's time as ague grass or ague root, though it was only the rootstock that was needed.

If fever is caused by sore throat or skin diseases such as erysipelas, they tried root tea made from black sanicle, often called black snakeroot, *Sanicula marilandica*. Even typhoid fever had a special plant remedy, a tea from the root of the cardinal flower, *Lobelia cardinalis*. Administer it in small quantities because of its strength. *Lobelia inflata*, Indian tobacco, may have been brewed in the same way, as botanist Breck wrote in 1866: "Its virtues are so prized by some that we are almost led to suppose that it is a sovereign remedy for all diseases that flesh and blood are heir to."[2]

Measles and its accompanying fever was sometimes attacked by making the patient drink a root tea from purple prairie clover, *Petalostemon purpureus*, also called violet prairie clover or red tassel flower.

If you don't like to dig roots there were other remedies.

The fruits of the hops, *Humulus lupulus*, could be steeped and drunk, and the seeds of the wild columbine, *Aquilegia canadensis*, were crushed in hot water and drunk. The wild columbine most successful in fever treatment is also known as honeysuckle, red with yellow center, a brightly nodding spot of spurred beauty in woods and thickets. One finds it in the west as well as the east, in the Rocky Mountains and Black Hills with varieties in the plains.

A febrifuge that tasted like lemonade was made from the sticky berries of the staghorn sumac, *Rhus typhina*, with a small amount of water.

If you shake with the chills and fever of the ague, you might get a bit of wine and add the seeds and flowers of the Canada wood nettle, *Laportea canadensis*, mix well, and drink. It is supposed to help.

[2]Joseph Breck, *New Book of Flowers*. New York: Orange Judd and Co., 1866. p. 270.

Meadow rue
Thalictrum dasycarpum

If the fever was caused by such illnesses as measles or small-pox, a bark tea from honey locust, *Gleditsia triacanthos*, was drunk. Smallpox was treated by Indians at one time by wild crab apples, *Pyrus ioensis*. The pitcher plant, *Sarracenia purpurea*, was even familiarly called the smallpox plant or fevercup, but it has long been acknowledged as not of much value in medicine. No wonder smallpox swept through early Indian tribes like a raging forest fire when white men brought it! Other names for the pitcher plant include sidesaddle flower, huntsman's-cup, Indian cup, Indian pitcher, Adam's cup, forefather's-cup, Adam's pitcher, forefather's-pitcher, whippoorwill's-boot or -shoe, watches, flytrap, and meadow-cup.

A fever accompanying diarrhea would be better treated by drinking bark tea made from winterberry, *Ilex verticillata*, but be sure you use the bark, not the berries.

We can go clear back to Roman times for a fever treatment by simmering the meadow anemone, *Anemone canadensis*, a plant containing a drug which was said to be valued by Romans for treating malarial fever. The Romans may have known another *Anemone*, more likely *A. vulgaris*. The *A. patens*, familiarly known as the pasqueflower, has been prepared by our own pioneers and others to increase perspiration, but we have no explicit directions. The lavender blossom can irritate if eaten.

In more modern times white men have peeled the inner bark of the button bush, *Cephalanthus occidentalis*, as a substitute for quinine.

A tonic brewed from the inner bark of the red ash, *Fraxinus pennsylvanica*, was drink to forestall recurring fevers, while bark tea from white ash, *F. americana*, treated the fever once it was established.

The *Mahonia* spp., Oregon grape and creeping hollygrape, were found to keep a fever from returning, the rhizome and roots dried and prepared as medicine. If these were not near, one could look for the roots of the spreading dogbane, *Apocynum androsaemifolium*, but the dogbane medicine was noted to be uncertain and irregular. It was taken with caution in well-guarded dosage.

The beautiful flowering dogwood of the southern states was valued for its dried root bark as a mild fever deterrent. This

180

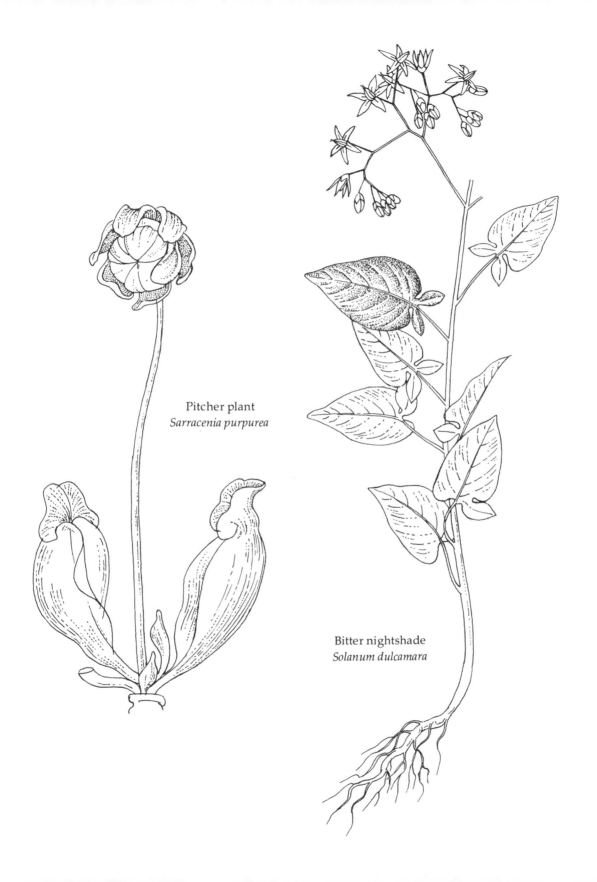

Pitcher plant
Sarracenia purpurea

Bitter nightshade
Solanum dulcamara

American elder
Sambucus canadensis

showy tree, *Cornus florida*, traditionally flowered just at the proper time for planting Indian corn, but there was no definite time for gathering the roots for medicinal use.

The bark and leaves of the quaking aspen, *Populus tremuloides*, made another brew for fever. The bark of the black willow, *Salix nigra*, contains salicin, a bitter principle used to lessen fever; and similarly bark was brewed from the American hornbeam, *Carpinus caroliniana*.

The bitter nightshade, *Solanum dulcamara*, whose berries were definitely inedible, could combat fever if one prepared it very precisely. Pick the young branches from plants only one or two years old, only after the leaves have fallen. From these young twigs they made a medicine that gives the plant one of its popular names, fevertwig. Other names for the plant are

182

Aspen
Populus tremuloides

bittersweet, climbing nightshade, woody nightshade, amara dulcis, blue bindweed, felonwort, poisonberry, poison flower, pushionberry, snakeberry, wolf grape, scarlet berry, tether-devil, dwale, and skawcoo.

The flowers of common elderberry, *Sambucus canadensis*, were dried, then steeped as a general fever medicine. In some areas one can more easily find the pink-petaled Philadelphia fleabane, *Erigeron philadelphicus*, the flowers of which were brewed to break a fever by causing the patient to sweat.

Find the white-flowering tops of the catnip, *Nepeta cataria*, if you would have another fever medicine. Catnip leaves have made a pleasant tea drink for centuries, but the medicinal value lies in the flowering tops and is said to produce a powerful perspiration that breaks the fever. Others that caused

183

Shell-leaf penstemon
Penstemon grandiflorus

the patient to sweat profusely included the elecampane, *Inula helenium*; and American spikenard, *Aralia racemosa*; from which one took the dried roots. A fairly familiar plant was the small yellow lady's-slipper, *Cypripedium calceolus* var. *parviflorum*, the roots of which were needed too. Yellow lady's-slipper blooms in early summer and may be difficult to find after that. The butterfly weed, *Asclepias tuberosa*, was almost as well known, being hunted for several illnesses besides for its faculty of making a patient break into a sweat.

Another plant tea of fever repute was made from the leaves of Canada mint, *Mentha arvensis* var. *villosa*. The tops of the slender Virginia mountain mint, *Pycnanthemum virginianum*, were simmered to combat the chills and fever of ague, or you could make a root tea from Culver's physic, *Veronicastrum virginicum*. The conspicuous white oxeye daisy, *Chrysanthemum leucanthemum*, was gathered and the whole plant simmered.

Tansy plant, *Tanacetum vulgare*, was a fever medicine causing one to perspire after the dryness of a feverish skin; or you could try leaf tea from eastern arborvitae, *Thuja occidentalis*. Intermittent fevers of undetermined origin were controlled by small skullcap, *Scutellaria parvula*, the whole plant being boiled for tea; by Oriental cocklebur, *Xanthium orientale*; and by the root of cup rosinweed, *Silphium perfoliatum*.

The Virginia creeper vine, *Parthenocissus quinquefolia*, is a brilliant red note of beauty in the autumn, but when the leaves are green they were plucked for a medicine to cool a body tossing in fever. The berries were said to be as effective when the leaves have fallen.

The shell-leaf penstemon, *Penstemon grandiflorus*, referred to as pink beardtongue, showy beardtongue, Canterbury bells, large-flowered beardtongue, or even wild foxglove, was said to be good for chills and fever, but one must steep the leaves for the beverage rather than the roots as we did in some flowers. The shell-leaf penstemon is a lovely plant. One can spot it a couple of hundred yards distant. It stands above the surrounding grass and lower flowers like a pink sentinel, and its color beckons with a bright gaiety.

The plant tops and leaves of boneset, *Eupatorium perfoliatum*; of heal-all or self-heal, *Prunella vulgaris*; and the leaves of the yarrow, *Achillea millefolium*, were also valued for fevers.

Boneset
Eupatorium perfoliatum

185

Bractless mentzelia
Mentzelia nuda

There were a few plants that could be applied externally to
allay fever. The bractless mentzelia, *Mentzelia nuda*, called prairie
lily or branched nuttalia, found on plains and hillsides west of the
Missouri River in the Dakotas, held its value in its stems. Strip
the stems of the leaves, and pound the stems to extract a gummy
yellow juice which must be boiled and strained. The liquid could
be applied externally, but we are left to guess where such
application would have most effect. The prairie lily is not
properly a lily, but a stickleaf. It has been called the white
evening star, though it blazons its creamy white blossom in the
late daytime too. This prairie beauty can grow from one to five
feet tall and is one of the few in its family to have winged
seeds.

186

Smooth alder
Alnus rugosa

More specific are the directions we find with the comments on big bluestem or red hay, *Andropogon gerardi*. If one is wounded and as a result of that wound one develops a fever, then gather the lower blades of this grass and apply them directly to the cut. Big bluestem is common on prairie land and easy to find if you know its appearance. It grows tall, three feet or more, with its spikelets in pairs.

In the Carolinas it was believed that jimsonweed, *Datura stramonium*, could be used to lower a fever just by applying the leaves to the body. Certainly one could not safely make a tea of the narcotic plant. Of less danger were leaves of alder, *Alnus rugosa*. It was said that if you put alder leaves in your night clothes against the body, they would lower your fever.

187

Wormwood
Artemisia glauca

Our last fever remedy is simplest of all. Find the wormwood, *Artemisia glauca*, also known as fuzzyweed, one of the sagebrushes of the plains area. Dip the whole plant in warm water and bathe with the plant.

Now that we think of it, not so many years ago when our oldest boy was burning with fever, our family physician advised bathing him in warm water (didn't mention fuzzyweed), and the fever cooled. Could the warm water have been enough in frontier days, too? This article not being a technical discussion, we are content to think of the sage as essential.

COLDS, NEURALGIA, AND RHEUMATISM

COLDS

*M*an has had colds for as long as he remembers. Probably the remedies of the frontiersmen didn't do much more good than the ones we have today, but at least they tried, and the mere effort to do something might have been comforting.

Other than the onion syrups discussed in the chapter on children's medicines, the cold remedy best remembered today is pennyroyal tea made from the leaves of the rough pennyroyal, *Hedeoma hispida*, an herb which grows on dry sandy soil over much of America. Steep the leaves and drink the beverage hot. They say the tea makes you break out in a perspiration that can be equaled only by catnip tea made from the flowering tops of catnip, *Nepeta cataria*. Rough pennyroyal tea is recommended primarily for colds, while catnip tea is also good for fever. After all, can we always separate the two? The plant is called rough pennyroyal, mock pennyroyal, squaw mint, thickweed, stinking balm, and mosquito plant, a low-growing plant six to twelve inches high with pale-blue flowers.

Many leaf teas were regarded as beneficial. Yarrow, *Achillea*

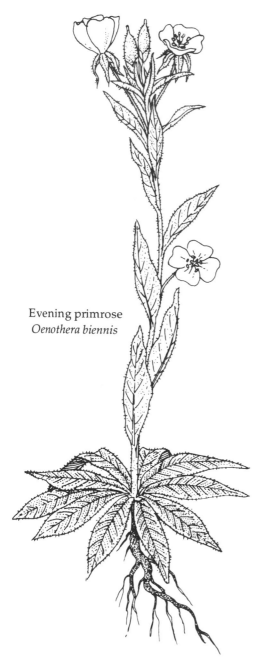

Evening primrose
Oenothera biennis

millefolium, that aromatic lacy foliage over meadows and hill-sides from coast to coast was one. The wild verbena or blue vervain, *Verbena hastata*, was noted by frontiersmen for reducing coughs. This blue-spiked flower of the wayside blooms all summer, but if we would make an herb tea for a winter cold we must pick the leaves and dry them to keep on hand.

Boneset, *Eupatorium perfoliatum*, made a tea that was fine for a cold, whether it lodged in the lungs, throat, or elsewhere. Leaf tea made from eastern arborvitae, *Thuja occidentalis*, was drunk for a cough or for bronchial catarrh; or if you have eastern hemlock tree, *Tsuga canadensis*, make a leaf tea and drink one full quart—bound to cure a cold, they say.

An extract was made from the leaves of bearberry, *Arctostaphylos uva-ursi*, for catarrh or chronic bronchitis. Either the leaves or the flowers or both could make a medicine to combat catarrh or bronchial infections when you have wild bergamot or bee balm, *Monarda fistulosa*. As often called horse-mint, the tea is said to combat any complications arising from a cold. Spotted bee balm, *M. punctata*, is also called horsemint, which may confuse the two, but don't worry. The spotted bee balm is a substitute.

If your patient has whooping cough, bad hiccoughs, or asthma, a prescription from the evening primrose plant, *Oenothera biennis*, will lessen the spasms of coughing or hic-coughing. It may not be a cure, but if it brings some comfort to the sufferer it is worth trying. The evening primrose has been known as night willow herb, large rampion, tree primrose, coffee plant, fever plant, king's cure-all, scurvish, and scabish.

The leaves of lion's-heart or false dragonhead, *Physostegia parviflora*, were steeped for a bad cold in the head. Call it either purple or western lion's-heart, too.

A leaf tea from the smooth hedge nettle, *Stachys tenuifolia*, was said to cure a cold. It has been called base horehound. The rosy twisted-stalk, *Streptopus roseus*, was boiled in its entirety for coughs. Other names for this were sessile-leaved twisted-stalk and liverberry.

Maidenhair fern, *Adiantum modestum* and *A. pedatum*, are two species that make a good cough syrup if you mix with honey. Of course we risk the skeptics who say that the honey by itself does the trick, and the maidenhair fern is just excess baggage.

Another syrup was made by boiling the fresh young leaves of horehound, *Marrubium vulgare*. Since the time of Pliny we have never really abandoned the horehound. Now it is available in horehound candy and cough drops, and can be added in many kinds of cookery. It is also called houndsbene, marvel, or marrube.

Several plants were gathered for their roots in making cold remedies one way or another. For instance, boil the roots of the speckled alder, *Alnus rugosa*, to make a cold medicine; or drink root tea from the blue flag, *Iris versicolor*, if you will remember that the iris root can act as a purge as well.

Small doses of the partially dried corm of jack-in-the-pulpit, *Arisaema triphyllum*, were tried in treating bronchitis, asthma, or related cold symptoms, though the jack-in-the-pulpit corm was recognized as a strong medicine to be taken very discreetly.

Another of more danger than good was the boiled root of the white wild indigo, *Baptisia leucantha*, which treated catarrh or chronic cold symptoms. Some people included the leaves in the wild indigo brew, and it was generally conceded that it increased respiration up to a point. Too much of the stuff could produce death by respiratory paralysis, a result not intended by the patient at all.

Root tea from small Solomon's seal, *Polygonatum biflorum*, eased a cough. This was the hairy Solomon's seal, sealwort, dwarf Solomon's seal, or conquer-john. Another root tea for coughs was boiled from wild sarsaparilla, *Aralia nudicaulis*, which was quite popular too.

Canada sagebrush, *Artemisia canadensis*, was mixed with angelica root; or the prairie sagebrush, *A. frigida*, was steeped by itself. The prairie sagebrush is a silvery feathery plant of singular appearance, sometimes called pasture sagebrush, estafiata, arctic, mountain sagebrush, wild sagebrush, worm sage, fringed wormwood, wormwood sage, or just wild sage.

Small doses of the bloodroot, *Sanguinaria canadensis*, would not only cause sneezing, but also loosened the accumulated phlegm in one's nose or throat. Remember to make the dose extremely small if you value your health. An overdose can kill you.

The calamus root, *Acorus calamus*, might taste better. At least

Hedge nettle
Stachys tenuifolia

Red cedar
Juniperus virginiana

its common name, sweet flag, sounds better. The long sword-shaped leaves are its trademark of appearance, but the root is what we want. The creeping woody rhizome is remembered today in parts of the world for the ague or intestinal ills, but for a cold we will want an infusion of the pounded root stock. Chew the root for a raw throat, or singers may chew it to clear the voice. If the cold plagues the whole head, then there is nothing left to do but to burn the root and breathe the smoke fumes as an inhalant.

There were several ways to make inhalants believed to help a cold in the head or in the chest. Since one breathed the remedy, it was assumed to go closer to the base of the illness. Chief among them was the smoke treatment made from several plants, including the calamus. Red cedar, *Juniperus virginiana*, is another excellent one. By "burning twigs and the head being enveloped in a blanket,"[1] one could inhale the smoke full strength. The red cedar was held in high esteem, and a dandy cough medicine could be made by boiling the fruits of the red cedar tree and its leaves together, then drinking.

Toast the tiny cones of the low birch, *Betula pumila*, on a plate of coals, inhaling the fumes — a treatment said to be effective against the most chronic nose inflammations.

The low poppy mallow, *Callirrhoë involucrata*, can be adapted to the smoke treatment too. For the cold in the head, burn the plant with your head under the blanket. Something ought to happen, that's sure.

Try the seeds of the Virginia anemone or thimbleweed, *Anemone virginiana*, for the chronic cold symptoms of catarrh, by inhaling the fumes when toasted. One more plant is a smoke treatment plant, that called by the botanical name *Silphium perfoliatum*, and by the common names cup plant, square-stem, angle stem, and rosinweed. This is not the same plant as its close cousin, *Silphium laciniatum*, also called rosin-weed, compass plant, pilotweed, or gumweed. The *S. laciniatum* is a general tonic, but for the smoke treatment we must find the *S. perfoliatum*. The difference between the two is slight. Both are members of the sunflower family, tall yellow-

[1]Melvin R. Gilmore, *Uses of Plants by the Indians of the Missouri River Region*. Bureau of American Ethnology report 1911–1912. Washington, D.C.: Government Printing Office, 1919. p. 63.

Anemone
Anemone virginiana

Eastern white pine
Pinus strobus

headed monarchs of the fields. *S. laciniatum* has deeply cut leaves with narrow lobes, and the other has less divided leaves. Unless you have a botanist's handbook with you it may be difficult to know which rosinweed is which.

Fumes could be created without smoke from several plants. For centuries the cultivated garlic, *Allium sativum*, has yielded a commercially extracted medicinal oil to counteract bronchitis, or the bruised bulbs can be a poultice in treating pneumonia, both types of illnesses connected to one's vague definition of a cold.

A powerful remedy for colds or bronchial ailments could be made from butter-and-eggs, *Linaria vulgaris*. First fix the hot water for a good sweat bath, then take the dried plant, mix with other foliage used in cold treatments, boil together, and

194

inhale the fumes while you are in the sweat bath. Something should give, if you can stand it.

The fumes were the healing agent in another remedy. One must grind the root of the false Solomon's seal, *Smilacina racemosa*, and soak and heat the liquid on a hot stove, inhaling the steam for colds or catarrhal ailments.

Buds, flowers, fruits, seeds, or bark of other plants or trees made remedies. Tree barks included the eastern larch or tamarack, *Larix laricina*, of which one steeped the inner bark for chronic bronchitis and drank; or dry the tamarack leaves, pulverize them, and inhale to treat the same bronchitis.

The bark of white pine, *Pinus strobus*, made a basis for a cough syrup. A bark tea good for a bad cold was that made from honey locust, *Gleditsia triacanthos*, using the twig bark only. You can call the honey locust by other names in some localities — sweet locust, three-thorned acacia, thorn locust, honey, honey chucks, or sweet bean.

The bark of slippery elm, *Ulmus rubra*, has been added to cough drops for its soothing quality, or has been made into a tea drunk for bronchial diseases.

If you could find it, bark from the plane tree or American sycamore, *Platanus occidentalis*, could be boiled as a cold medicine. More familiarly it is known in backyard conversation as buttonwood, buttonball, or false sycamore.

The buds of three poplar trees were considered valuable, giving us a different remedy for a cold in the head by boiling balm of Gilead buds in fat to make a salve which we put up the nostrils. Also called balsam poplar or balm buds, X *Populus gileadensis*, the buds attacked deeper lung infections too. The same salve was made from the southern poplar called balsam poplar, *Populus deltoides* var. *missouriensis*, treating colds, catarrh, bronchitis, and related respiratory congestions. Other names for the tree are Carolina poplar, Ontario poplar, and rough bark poplar.

The buds of the quaking aspen, *Populus tremuloides*, that dancing tree of the hill country, were cooked in fat to make a like salve for nasal application to cure coughs and colds. The bark and leaves were boiled for a medicinal tea for colds or hay fever, influenza, or whatever resembled a cold. Some know it as trembling aspen, American aspen, quiverleaf, American

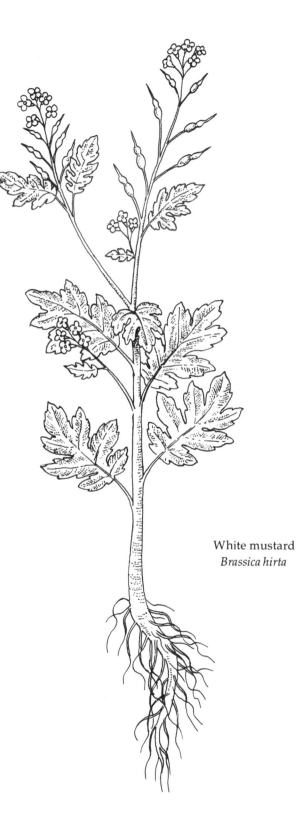

White mustard
Brassica hirta

poplar, trembling poplar, white poplar, quaking asp, or mountain asp.

Balsam gum from the balsam fir, *Abies balsamea*, was applied directly from the trunk blisters for colds or other pulmonary troubles, or the leaves of the balsam fir were smoked and inhaled for a cold.

A simple cough medicine was made by boiling the bark of the pin cherry tree, *Prunus pensylvanica*, called wild red cherry, or the bark of the black cherry tree, *P. serotina*; but about the most pleasant cold remedy we have encountered is the recipe for hot buttered rum from the fruit of the black or rum cherry tree. Make your rum, sweeten with maple syrup from the sugar maple tree, heat, add butter, and sip gratefully for any deep-seated cold. The main problem in this recipe would seem to be the gathering of enough black cherries to make the rum, since they are a favorite tidbit for seventy kinds of birds who will get there first if they can.

If we are hoarse, not really in bed with a cold, we are reminded that we might try the fruits of the greenbrier, *Smilax herbacea*. Inasmuch as the greenbrier is also called carrion flower because of its putrid scent, we think we might enjoy the hoarseness more, but everyone is entitled to his own taste. The berries are blue-black when ripe.

If you don't have bark, buds, or fruit, you could try seeds or flower heads. The seeds of the Virginia penthorum, the ditch or Virginia stonecrop, *Penthorum sedoides*, were crushed to make a cough syrup of particular use in treating deep-seated catarrhal colds.

For a simple cold in the head, grind the seeds of black mustard, *Brassica nigra*, or white mustard, *B. hirta*, a cultivated mustard, and sniff the resultant powder into the nostrils in the manner of snuff.

The sneezeweed, *Helenium autumnale*, gets its name directly from its purpose. It is said that if you dried the flower heads, pulverized them, then snuffed the flower powder into the nostrils, they would make you sneeze—thus loosening a cold in the head to facilitate easier healing. For additional curative effects you could make a tea of the florets to drink, attacking the cold symptoms internally. A big yellow blossom, it is also known as false sunflower, swamp sunflower, and yellow star

Mullein
Verbascum thapsus

197

besides the descriptive name of staggerwort, which tells you what happens if you get too much of it.

If you have the yellow water crowfoot, *Ranunculus flabellaris*, you could take the center of the flowers or the stigmas and snuff them into the nostrils to cause sneezing, thereby loosening the cold. The blossom was sometimes used alone, sometimes mixed with others, but always as a powder inhalant.

One last suggestion—a cold in the head or the more severe symptoms of catarrh could sometimes be broken by sniffing the powdered disk florets of the pink Philadelphia fleabane, *Erigeron philadelphicus*, directly into the nostrils or by inhaling smoke from burning the dried blossoms. Here again, the sniffing of the powdered blossoms into the nostrils will cause sneezing to loosen the cold.

NEURALGIA AND RHEUMATISM

The bush morning-glory, *Ipomoea leptophylla*, brings us to one of the strangest chapters on prairie medicine. The roaming Indians had their share of aches and pains, we can be sure, and the frontiersmen and women were right with them. The redmen may not have called their miseries such dignified names as neuralgia and rheumatism, but they hurt just the same and they had to do something about it. What they did was generally amazing.

The bush morning-glory treatment was one of the simpler remedies for rheumatism. If their legs and shoulders ached they dried one of its roots, pulverized it, and rubbed the dust on the pain. Does it disappear? Personally we have never had rheumatism and can't say.

Primitive remedies for rheumatic pains included steam baths besides the smoke treatment, a medieval torture called moxa, counterirritants, tea solutions that were either drunk or washed on the aching limbs, poultices, and finally special bath solutions.

They knew two plants which they believed to be beneficial in the smoke treatment for vague achings. The prairie thermopsis, *Thermopsis rhombifolia*, called false lupine, golden pea, yellow pea, or bush pea, was one. They gathered the bright

Prairie thermopsis
Thermopsis rhombifolia (photograph: Marjorie Morcom)

sunshiny-yellow blossoms, dried them, and smoked them. We have seen acres of prairie thermopsis blooming in the springtime coloring a whole hillside like spilled paint. It is a sight to be remembered.

The other plant is cup plant, *Silphium perfoliatum*. The smoke of the cup plant root is said to ease neuralgic pains as well as a cold in the head, though you could also make a tea from its root to drink for lumbago or rheumatic pains in the back. The rosinweed, *S. integrifolium*, had a painkilling property that made life easier for cripples, too, though the root was steamed in a hole with the steam directed at the seat of pain in a crippled body, not only relieving the pain but also supposedly aiding in healing. The root of the compass plant, *S. laciniatum*, was boiled for a beverage against rheumatism.

Here's one for you. If you have rheumatism to the point of numbness or near paralysis, ask a friend to help you in a steam bath. Get in a tent or small enclosure of some kind, in the middle of which set a pot of water boiling. Throw in the branches and roots of Canada yew, *Taxus canadensis*, called American yew, dwarf yew, shinwood, or creeping hemlock. Once they have boiled a bit, toss in some hot stones and get as close to the steam as you can. Take our word, it was once done.

Now that we have disposed of the two less surprising ways of treating rheumatic miseries we'll go on to the drastic ones. If that dadgummed pain persists despite all you can do, then we can make a moxa.

The moxa was built by breaking short pieces of stems of certain plants, attaching them to the skin by moistening one end with the tongue, then setting fire to the other end. The stems are allowed to burn down to the skin, and the pains of neuralgia or rheumatism leave in self-defense, we assume.

Leadplant or shoestring, *Amorpha canescens*, also called wild tea, was one of the first to secure if possible. The leadplant is a brushy plant with lavender florets that give it an unexpected beauty during the blossoming period. This is a dry plains plant growing on rolling prairies or low foothills.

Roundhead lespedeza, rabbitfoot or bush clover, *Lespedeza capitata*, could be stripped of its close-growing leaves and its heavy cream-colored petals made into moxa. One tall stalk

Buttercup
Ranunculus sp.

Aromatic aster
Aster oblongifolius

growing about three feet high would probably be all we could stand of the treatment anyway.

The prairie aster, *Aster oblongifolius* in particular, is fine for moxa too. We would much rather gather its pretty blossoms for a wild bouquet to place on the hall table and just sit with our rheumatism and look at it.

The more we think of moxa, the less we think of it, as a matter of fact. Could the counterirritant be any worse?

The counterirritant method is produced by finding plants that are rubbed on the sore spots, which thereupon produce blisters that hurt worse than the original pain, so in the end one can forget the first for the second. The theory is that when the second pain goes, it takes the first with it.

Jack-in-the-pulpit, *Arisaema triphyllum*, has already been gathered for its powers in curing a headache, so we might as

201

well rub what was left of the pulverized corm dust on our
rheumatism to see if it works as well as they claim. Rub well,
and wait. Which pain would you rather have?

Two crowfoots or buttercups were counterirritants. The
mud-rooted Pennsylvania buttercup or bristly crowfoot,
Ranunculus pennsylvanicus, was valued for its irritating seeds,
but the blister buttercup called cursed crowfoot, *R. sceleratus*,
raised a better blister and therefore commanded more respect.
The blister buttercup has also been called rogue buttercup or
desert crowfoot. Root bark of the smooth sumac, *Rhus glabra*,
raised a blister of less power.

We regret exceedingly to have to report that spring's delicate
beauty, the spreading pasqueflower, can also be a counterirritant. Crush leaves and apply. A blister will appear, you may be
sure. We are even warned "dangerous if taken internally,"[2]
but we had no intention of eating it. The spreading pasqueflower has more names than you can imagine, and there it sits
modest and unassuming and so cheerful in spite of its bur-
dens, peeking out of the last of the snow with its fur coat
covering its stems and leaves. Botanically it is the *Anemone
patens*, but its popular names vary with every state, or sometimes with every county. The Indians had names for it that did
not meet the white men's names, and all were lovely names.
We knew it first as the crocus, but it is also called the mayflower, Easter flower, windflower, prairie anemone, American
pulsatilla, hartshorn, headache plant, blue tulip, lion's beard,
gosling, badger, April fool, prairie smoke, and rock lily. The
early Dakota Indian name for it was *Hokshi-chekpa wahcha*,
which translated to "twin flower." Gentle little crocus, friend
of my childhood, what has become of you, lost in this labyrinth
of names?

If you don't like counterirritants, you can find something to
drink. Bud resin from the sticky fragrance of the balm of Gilead
poplar tree, X *Populus gileadensis*, eased rheumatism, the
medicine being made by soaking a crock full of buds in alcohol
and administering the medicine sparingly by mouth. Both the
balm of Gilead poplar and the southern poplar, *Populus
deltoides* var. *missouriensis*, could be handled thus; though the

[2]Gilmore, *Uses of Plants*, p. 82.

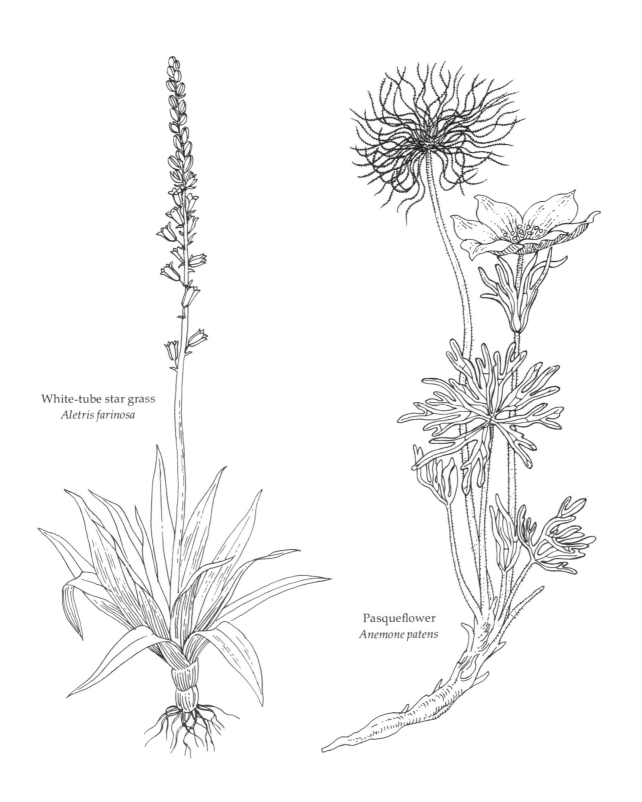

White-tube star grass
Aletris farinosa

Pasqueflower
Anemone patens

bark and leaves of the quaking aspen, *P. tremuloides*, were
steeped in water to be drunk for rheumatic pains.

Can we call alfalfa a wild plant? It is extensively cultivated in
the plains states as an important forage food, but undoubtedly
it has escaped and grows wild in the most unexpected places.
This purple-blooming member of the pea family, *Medicago
sativa*, is still known by old-timers as an excellent tea for
rheumatism, neuralgia, any kind of ache or pain. They dry
leaves, blossoms, and stems, and make a hot brew of the dried
bits. If you do not know the alfalfa, be sure you do not confuse
it with one of the purple-blossomed species of astragalus or
locoweed, the tea of which would certainly do you no good.
Stay away from the *Astragalus* spp., but do not hesitate to use
the alfalfa if it strikes your fancy. Alfalfa has various common
names, including purple medic, nonesuch, lucerne, Burgundy
clover, Chilian clover, Brazilian clover, snail clover, holy hay,
and sainfoin.

A similar result can be had by drinking the dried leaves and
flowering tops of the yellow sweet clover, *Melilotus officinalis*,
that sweet-smelling weed that grows like crazy wherever it is
started.

The dried rhizome and roots of white-tube star grass,
Aletris farinosa, were also thought to combat rheumatism, and
one would assume that the roots should be brewed for the
liquid, possibly just to wash on the aching parts. Admittedly
the starry silene or starry campion, *Silene stellata*, was a wash
for aches, sprains and sores.

A bark tea held in the mouth to combat neuralgia in the face
was made from gray dogwood, *Cornus racemosa*. Root tea from
horse gentian, *Triosteum perfoliatum*, was good for rheumatism;
or you could try eastern arborvitae, *Thuja occidentalis*, for a
simpler leaf tea rheumatism remedy.

A root tea from any of the anemones, *Anemone* spp., was
believed by some to be good for rheumatism and ridiculed by
others.

Try root tea from burdock, *Arctium minus*, or maybe a tea
made from the whole plant of the small green shepherd's
purse, *Capsella bursa-pastoris*.

One tea that was definitely drunk for rheumatism was from
the checkerberry or wintergreen, *Gaultheria procumbens*. This is

Racemose milkweed (sometimes called locoweed)
Astragalus racemosa

Alfalfa
Medicago sativa

understandable, as wintergreen was once the source of methyl salicylate, approximately the same active principle which is incorporated into aspirin. Once an important source, it is no longer a commercial source of salicylic acid. Wintergreen oil was added to liniments, but one was cautioned against an overdose of the pure oil on the skin as detrimental in some cases, producing drowsiness, congestion, and even delirium.

Spotted cranesbill, *Geranium maculatum*, was made into a root tea for neuralgia, or anything to do with soreness in the jaws; but for rheumatic pains over the body you could try a root tea from American twinleaf, *Jeffersonia diphylla*, so recognized that one of the common names of the twinleaf is rheumatism root. It is also known as helmetpod, ground-squirrel pea, and yellowroot.

The leaves of peppermint, *Mentha piperita*, made a sedative beverage, or the fresh leaves were applied over local pains for

205

relief. Root tea from mayapple or mandrake, *Podophyllum peltatum*, treated rheumatism among other maladies. The little purple monkshood, *Aconitum* spp., sometimes called wolfbane, is ordinarily regarded as poisonous but it is said that the drug aconite, an arterial and nerve sedative, can be obtained from the roots to treat sciatica and other neuralgias. Milder treatments for neuralgia included the leaves of horseradish, *Armoracia lapathifolia*; and lady fern, *Athyrium filix-femina*, for backache.

If you are really crippled, you could always try stiff tickseed, *Coreopsis palmata*. Either boil the seeds and drink the brew, or make a poultice of the boiled seeds to put over the painful area, or do both at the same time.

Joe-pye weed, *Eupatorium purpureum*, was made into a root solution for rheumatism and the pains of gout, but one is not certain whether it should be drunk or used as a wash. Lumbago and rheumatism would sometimes react favorably to a plaster made from the bark and pitch of eastern hemlock, *Tsuga canadensis*. Of course you can always make a mustard plaster. Gather the seeds of the tall black mustard, *Brassica nigra*, or the white mustard, *B. hirta*, and flax, *Linum lewisii*. Grind them and mix with hog fat or mutton tallow. Having no hogs or sheep handy, maybe ordinary shortening would answer as well. Some mustard plasters called for a recipe of ground mustard seed mixed with equal quantities of flour if the flaxseed meal was not available, then moistened with lukewarm water rather than the hog fat or mutton tallow. Both black and white mustard are European imports that have been cultivated, escaped, grown wild, and are still cultivated. Black mustard is also recognized as red mustard, brown mustard, cadlock, kerlock, and scurvy-senvy; the white mustard shares the name senvy besides being called yellow mustard, charlock, and kidlock.

A poultice by which our early Americans set great store was made by cooking the roots of the purple-stem angelica, *Angelica atropurpurea*, pounding them to a pulp, mixing them with the bruised leaves of Canada sagebrush, *Artemisia canadensis*, and slapping the hot plaster to the side of the body opposite the pain — any pain at all. The plaster would also reduce swellings. Purple-stem angelica was known as Ameri-

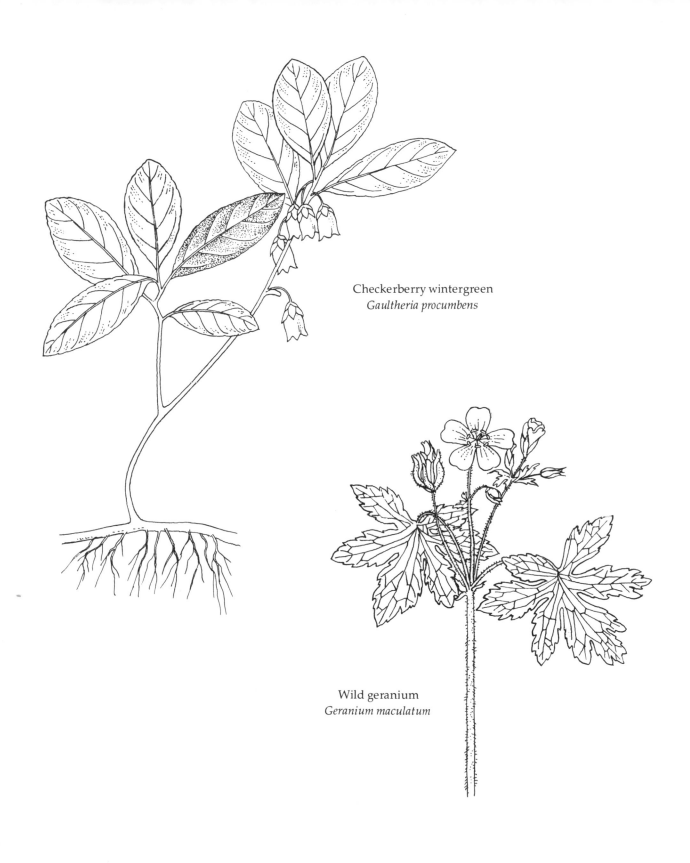

Checkerberry wintergreen
Gaultheria procumbens

Wild geranium
Geranium maculatum

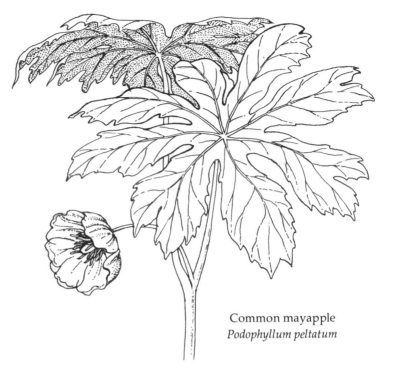

Common mayapple
Podophyllum peltatum

can angelica, great angelica, high angelica, and masterwort, an
obvious plant that sometimes grew six feet tall.

Another poultice was made from dried flowers of the common elder, *Sambucus canadensis*. Though pharmacists claimed
elder poultice had little value, it enjoyed a vogue among some
people.

A soothing liquid to be washed over the rheumatic areas was
made from a hot fomentation of mayweed or camomile flowers, *Anthemis cotula*, known also as dog fennel, with water and
vinegar; or sweet fern, *Comptonia peregrina*, made a fomentation
wash for general rheumatism.

We are comforted finally when we note one plant that can
help rheumatic pains simply by bathing. The false tarragon
sagebrush, *Artemisia glauca*, that good green sage, cooled a
fever when combined in bathing with warm water, and the
same treatment can be given for rheumatism. Just lie back,
relax, let the sagebrush take the pains away and forget all else.
Sounds wonderful. This one might be worth trying.

208

GENERAL TONICS

$\mathcal{M}$ ention of big bluestem, *Andropogon Gerardi*, reminds us that a medicine for general debility is said to be made from the lower blades of the grass, but we are not sure just how. Too bad—we need some almost any day.

A stack of others were known as tonics to boost flagging energy. Let's take a look at them and see if any seem right for the twentieth-century run-down feeling.

How about the gentian? Botanists refer to one as the *Gentiana puberula*, more commonly known as the downy gentian. This pretty blue tubular flower is found in damp grasslands. It does seem a shame to pick them, but if we want their medicinal values we must pull them, roots and all, to make a tea of the root. The upper plant is worthless except for a table decoration but its beauty might do us more good in that way than the root, after all. Some say the fringed gentian, *G. crinita*, was best, but the fringed gentian is becoming too rare a flower to be killed so haphazardly.

For loss of appetite or just aiding the digestion, the root of the Andrews or closed gentian, *Gentiana andrewsi*, was eaten; or the root of the five-leaved gentian called stiff gentian, five-flowered gentian, gall of the earth, or gallweed, *G. quinquefolia*. Keep the quantity small if you drink root tea made from small Solomon's seal, *Polygonatum biflorum*, to increase your appetite,

209

Small Solomon's seal
Polygonatum biflorum

210

which might be better encouraged by a bark tea from American hornbeam or blue beech, *Carpinus caroliniana*. Loss of appetite is no joke in any generation. If you can't eat there's something the matter with you and you'd better look for hornbeam tea or gentian tea or anything else that will help. In southern states a small dose of wild cherry bark scraped fine and stewed in a bottle with whiskey for several days gave an ailing person a wonderful appetite.

A tonic taken to change almost any condition for the better was made from the root of the moonseed, *Menispermum canadense*. The berries of the moonseed are poisonously narcotic but the root contains bitter alkaloids that suited our medicine makers just fine. It is also known as Canada moonseed, yellow parilla, Texas sarsaparilla, yellow sarsaparilla, and vine maple, the last name referring to the resemblance its leaves have to maple leaves, though they can look like wild grape leaves to the uninitiated.

Any sickness at all can be treated by a root bark tea from the roots of red mulberry, *Morus rubra*. Any sickness? That's what the old-timers said.

The sweet cicely, *Osmorhiza longistylis*, was also good for everything, a particularly fine medicine to help you regain flesh and strength after an illness if you mix the leaves with the bark of honey locust, *Gleditsia triacanthos*, to make a beverage.

There were a number of plants that were said to be good for what ailed you, no matter what it was. The bark of the toothache tree, *Zanthoxylum clavaherculis*, was one, hot-tasting though it may be. Just peel a chunk of toothache tree bark and chew.

Culver's physic, *Veronicastrum virginicum*, was believed to be a good reviver if eaten, but one wonders why when it is also known to be a strong emetic. Culver's physic isn't too easy to find, but everyone knows how to spot the red clover, *Trifolium pratense*, which has a fairly good reputation as a curative agent in its dried blossoms brewed in a tea. The dried root of sarsaparilla, *Smilax medica*, was popularly believed to be a tonic of sorts.

There's no accounting for tastes. Pokeberry root is known to be poisonous, yet there were those who said that if you collected the dried root in the autumn it could make you well.

Eucalyptus
Eucalyptus globulus

Since pokeweed root can cause all sorts of reactions, one would hesitate now to test it.

Cohosh bugbane, *Cimicifuga racemosa*, that tall slender-stemmed plant, has a thick rootstalk that has been dug for a medication to make one feel better. The dried rhizome and roots of American spikenard, *Aralia racemosa*, are also said to give a sick person a boost toward health again.

There were stimulating tonics for that fagged feeling. You may not be really sick, but sort of run down. You need a little energy or just a good night's sleep or something. Then is when you would look into the possibilities of the stimulating tonics. One such was the dried fruit of the caraway, *Carum carvi*, found in gardens or escaped into the wild state. Virginia or Texas snakeroot, *Aristolochia serpentaria*, was another, but the dried rhizome and roots, were used.

The seeds of either white or black mustard, *Brassica hirta* and *B. nigra*, made a stimulant, too, even as we put a dash of mustard into our cooking today for its flavor. The flowers of marigold, *Calendula officinalis*, were prettier, and there were those who said the dried florets were also better than the mustard seed as a stimulant. Marigold could be found in the garden as often as not.

The root of the Alaska goldthread, *Coptis groenlandica*, was a mild tonic; as was the dried bark of the sweetwood, *Croton eluteria*, a sweet-smelling bark. The dried leaves collected from the older parts of the eucalyptus tree, *Eucalyptus globulus*, were picked as a stimulant; but if one wanted to use the eastern wahoo, *Euonymus atropurpureus*, he had to dry the bark of the root and make a tonic from that. Pharmacy books list the wahoo bark too, but caution that its tonic is uncertain and irregular. One must guard the dosage carefully.

Common fennel, *Foeniculum vulgare*, yielded a volatile oil prepared from the dried ripe fruit as a stimulant of fairly good flavor. Sometimes our ancestors believed that medicine should taste rather awful if it were to have any value, so there were those that swore by the efficacy of the dried bark of the ash, *Fraxinus* spp., because it made such a bitter tonic. The dried rhizome and roots of the yellow gentian, *Gentiana lutea*, ran a close second in the bitter-tasting field.

Spotted geranium, *Geranium maculatum*, was handy for a

Eucalyptus leaves
Eucalyptus globulus

213

Wild rose
Rosa sp.

variety of ailments, so it is no wonder that it was also pulled from the ground to make a root tonic as well. Perhaps camomile tea made from the dried flower heads of the camomile, *Matricaria chamomilla*, was better known as a stimulating tonic.

Anise, *Pimpinella anisum*, was fairly well known as a stimulant, but perhaps the most pleasant tonic was that made from rose petals. *Rosa gallica*, the red rose, was particularly noted for its tonic qualities; the dried petals were collected just before the expansion of the flower for best results. In fact, red rose petals made a splendid addition to many medicines, just for the flavor or scent as the case may be.

At least two of the docks, *Rumex crispus*, curled dock, and *R. obtusifolius*, yellow dock or bitter dock, have been gathered for a root tonic; and black haw, *Viburnum prunifolium*, has been searched for its bark to be dried and steeped.

Taken in small doses, bogbean or buckbean, *Menyanthes trifoliata*, will make you feel better. Increase the dose and you have something else.

An astringent tonic was made from roots and leaves of the Canada wood nettle, *Laportea canadensis*, by boiling, then drinking the concoction. The root of the smooth sumac, *Rhus glabra*, was boiled for a beverage; or the root of the pitcher plant, *Sarracenia purpurea*, was boiled to make a mild tonic admitted to be of inconclusive value.

The root of horse gentian, *Triosteum perfoliatum*, was prepared so generally for convalescence from fevers that it acquired the popular names of feverwort and feverroot, among others. It made a drink to cleanse the system, and was believed to help various specific ailments as well.

Only very recently we learned that the roots of the Oregon grape and creeping hollygrape, *Mahonia aquifolium* and *M. repens*, are known as a tonic brew today. The leatherflower, *Clematis viorna*, is a great deal harder to find than the Oregon grape, but if you find it you could make a like dosage by boiling the root, and one fewer leatherflower will make the flower even more difficult to locate. Wild cucumber root or wild balsam apple, *Echinosystis lobata*, will do the job as well— or use burdock. The roots of the burdocks, either *Arctium minus* or *A. lappa*, made a medicine said to justify it's existence.

215

That strange flower the compass plant, *Silphium laciniatum*,
from which primitive children extracted their chewing gum,
had a certain value for their parents, too. Beyond the fact that
the leaves have a tendency to point northward and southward,
settlers knew its root could be boiled to combat a jaded feeling.
This is a prairie flower, and if you once differentiate it from the
others you will have an interesting plant on your hands. Other
Silphium species were similar, including the root of the entire-
leaved rosinweed, *S. integrifolium*, which was known to be a
painkiller and therefore was doubly valued as a stimulating
drink as well. If pain goes, one naturally feels better. The root
of the cup plant, *S. perfoliatum*, was said to change anything for
the better—ulcers, liver affections, general debility.

Purple meadow rue, *Thalictrum dasycarpum*, made a root tea
that was a booster drunk to prevent the recurrence of illnesses.
If a child had been sick but gave indications of improving, for
example — quick, give him a dose of meadow rue tea! Let's
keep him getting better if possible!

If meadow rue wasn't handy, find the root of the purple-
stem angelica, *Angelica atropurpurea*. We would bet our bottom
dollar, if our own experience is worth anything, that the
average person would be more likely to find meadow rue than
purple-stem angelica.

A very mild tonic was made from the root of the Canada
wild ginger, *Asarum canadense*. A general tonic recognized for
specific ailments as well was made from leaves of pipsissewa,
Chimaphila umbellatum, which were also added to other mix-
tures to make them taste better.

Leaves were specified in several ways. One of the more
appetizing may have been cowslip wine made from the cowslip
or marsh marigold, *Caltha palustris*. We are sorry, we do not
have the recipe. If you are desperate maybe you could substitute a general uplifter made from the golden groundsel, *Senecio
aureus*, and the lamb's-tongue groundsel, *S. integerrimus*, but
we do not advise it. Groundsel side reactions can be bad!

There are plenty of people in the United States today who
have heard that the leaves of boneset or thoroughwort,
Eupatorium perfoliatum, can make an excellent tonic, though it
must be taken in small doses for that purpose. Because its
opposite leaves are so united that the stem seems to be pierc-

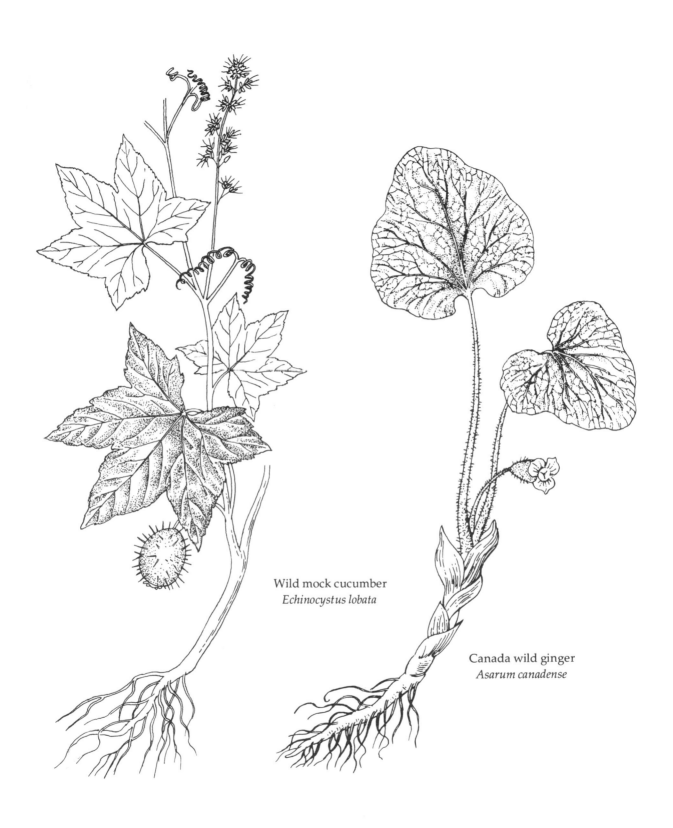

Wild mock cucumber
Echinocystus lobata

Canada wild ginger
Asarum canadense

Creeping hollygrape
Mahonia repens

ing through a common leaf, it was once believed to have curative effects in healing fractured bones.

Tansy, *Tanacetum vulgare,* made a cold infusion said to be fine for aiding convalescence from exhausting diseases, dyspepsia, hysteria, or jaundice, although overdoses could make the patient considerably worse than he was when he started his course of tansy medication.

Boil the aromatic leaves of the yarrow or milfoil, *Achillea millefolium,* or the dried cones of the hop, *Humulus lupulus,* for beverages that would have a different taste. We have not tried either, but the yarrow is easy to find and today the cultivated hops are a well-known ingredient of a popular pick-me-up — beer.

You've been quite sick and your illness left you weak in your convalescence. What you need to perk you up to your normal verve is a tea made from the needles of red cedar, *Juniperus virginiana.* Boil the needles well to get all the goodness from them. A similar tea was made from the dried leaves of the fragrant goldenrod, *Solidago odora,* called by several names such as sweet goldenrod, woundweed, blue mountain tea, sweet-scented goldenrod, anise-scented goldenrod, and true goldenrod.

Thistle tonic had its day as a good-for-what-ails-you tonic, being made from the dried plants of Canada thistle, *Cirsium arvense;* bull thistle, *C. vulgare;* and field thistle, *C. discolor.* If you were just run down, perhaps a little tired, a leaf tea from the dainty Virginia mountain mint could help. This slender plant, *Pycnanthemum virginianum,* is modest and small, but you can find it if you look. If you cannot, then borrow the leaves of the spotted touch-me-not, *Impatiens capensis.*

Wild Virginia strawberry leaves made a tea for pleasure drinking, but if you want a strengthening drink use the root of the strawberry, *Fragaria virginiana.*

The bitter taste of salicin in black willow, *Salix nigra,* was said to cure humans at times as well as tanning leather. Called swamp willow, scythe-leaved willow, and pussy willow, this is a wide ragged tree of the countryside found most often leaning over stream banks.

The bark of the pear hawthorn, *Crataegus calpodendron,* was boiled for that weak feeling, but if you had some kind of an

219

Red cedar
Juniperus virginiana

indefinite pain in the side you made the pear hawthorn tea from the twigs. Don't ask us why, just simmer those twigs.

You may steep the inner bark of the hazel alder, *Alnus rugosa*, called common alder, tag alder, American alder, or green alder, for a medicine that should bring back your general health after a period of illness; or steep the bark of black cherry, *Prunus serotina*, which was a good tonic for general debility besides being a tea tasty enough to be drunk with meals just to add its flavor.

Winterberry, *Ilex verticillata*, occasionally provided a general bark tea medication, more specifically for stomach or bowel upsets.

When scurvy was recognized as a dietary deficiency several plants were thought to be of value, some of them being the root of the red and yellow columbine, *Aquilegia canadensis*; the buds of the quaking aspen, *Populus tremuloides*; and an infusion made from the Virginia pepperweed, *Lepidium virginicum*, called wild peppergrass and bird's-pepper. Bud resin from balm of Gilead poplar, *X Populus gileadensis*, was not only protection against scurvy but also made a good stimulating general tonic. Southern poplar, *Populus deltoides* var. *missouriensis*, or balm of Gilead poplar were better when the diagnosis was purely scurvy.

The bright-yellow dandelion, *Taraxacum officinale*, that bane of our front yards and darling of our children's hearts, has been said to have medical qualities of all sorts during the centuries. It can be listed under a number of illnesses if one desires, but its healing properties are so vaguely defined (generally hiding behind lists of big names that mean more or less the same things) that it seems best to call it simply a general tonic. The milky white juice contains the healing properties, and can be a gentle laxative, a blood purifier, a cure for liver complaint, a remedy for indigestion — name it, we have it. Worded simply, the dandelion plant is said to change one's health for the better. Worded very simply, it's good for you. So said the old-timers.

Catnip, *Nepeta cataria*, made a leaf tea that is one of the oldest beverages drunk as a general tonic, dating from earliest days in Europe and introduced to America with the colonists. It was adopted enthusiastically by American Indians and is enjoyed by Indians and whites today from one end of the country to the other. One of the beliefs connected with it is that it gave courage and strength to one who drank the brew. This perennial has heart-shaped leaves with whitish spikes of flowers. catmint could be thrown into a lukewarm bath to raise the purifier for the blood and to settle the stomach. Catnip or catmint could the thrown into a lukewarm bath to raise the body temperature if you had a chill, which naturally would make you feel better, too.

221

Leaves of the downy phlox, *Phlox pilosa*, would purify the blood as well. Steep the leaves and drink. The act of purifying the blood is a little hazy to our ears in this twentieth century. Was it just an important-sounding phrase, or did our ancestors believe that all sicknesses were in the blood (that is, saturated through the veins of the body) more than elsewhere? Did they consider the blood to be actually contaminated, or was it on the order of the old springtime recipe of sulphur and molasses to thin the blood after a long hard winter? Blood disorders existed then as now, of course, but the term "purifying the blood" somehow seems to be more of a graceful phrase than a medical term. Maybe the whole thing was psychological.

In any case, the directions remain.

Lacking access to phlox leaves, you could try tea made from mayweed camomile or dog fennel, *Anthemis cotula*; or bearberry, *Arctostaphylos uva-ursi*, for your impure blood. Other blood purifiers were leaf tea made from either the small cranberry, *Vaccinium oxycoccus*; or the blueberry, *V. angustifolium*. All of the violets were blood purifiers at one distant time, with particular emphasis being given to the white Canada violet, *Viola canadensis*, and the American dog violet, *Viola conspersa*. You could drink a tea from wild mint, American or Canada mint, *Mentha arvensis* var. *villosa*, or throw the mint leaves in a sweat bath and inhale while you were steaming.

Although leaf tea was made from eastern arborvitae, *Thuja occidentalis*, as a blood purifier, most trees were stripped of their bark for medicinal prescription. The American sycamore or plane tree, *Platanus occidentalis*, gave its bark. Besides purifying the blood as a general tonic, the sycamore was said to stop hemorrhages, too.

The bark of the alder, *Alnus rugosa*, was scraped and boiled, a tea given a tablespoonful at a time, three times a day, to purify the blood especially when carbuncles were present.

A root infusion of the dwarf bush honeysuckle, *Diervilla lonicera*, was once drunk to cure senility, surely a marvelous brew that might more appropriately be called magic. Though one of its common names was gravelweed, the name life-of-man came directly from this old belief.

Preventive medicine had a few followers. The root of the false Solomon's seal, *Smilacina racemosa*, was cooked with food

White prairie clover
Petalostemon candidum

in the belief that it would prevent plague among humans, or when mixed with hog food it would prevent hog cholera. White settlers had a more complicated reason for the false Solomon's seal. They said it strengthened the heart muscle, thereby increasing the blood pressure and stimulating respiration, all of which aided appetite and digestion.

The white prairie clover, *Petalostemon candidus*, could be added to our list. Unfortunately we must dig the root of this prairie clover, too, but if you put the pulverized root in hot water it makes a most healthful drink. Pshaw with this business of being sick—we'll drink white prairie clover tea instead.

223

Paper birch
Betula papyrifera

Offhand, can you think of a medicine that brings a reaction from you which can be described simply as "Ugh!"? In fact, it tastes awful? There probably would be a great many more such medicines than there are today if druggists hadn't made some effort in recent years to add pleasant flavorings. Cough syrups are a good example. Most cough syrups are given by mothers to their coughing youngsters, and all mothers know that if a syrup tastes good it is far easier to get down a child's throat. A boy can think of more ways to avoid the medicine than his mother can devise to make him take it.

Obviously the situation has existed for centuries if we can believe the old folktales of medicines. Several plants were mixed as a matter of course with other medical plants just to make the whole thing taste good. Any time during the year you could find balsam fir, *Abies balsamea*, for that purpose; the bearberry, *Arctostaphylos uva-ursi*; or the root of the paper birch, *Betula papyrifera*. Summertime would give you the root of the bull thistle, *Cirsium vulgare*; the leaves and tops of sweet fern, *Comptonia peregrina*; or leaves from checkerberry or wintergreen, *Gaultheria procumbens*. Another seasoner easier to find during the summer was the root of elecampane, *Inula helenium*, a plant known popularly as inula, inul, horsehead, elf dock, elfwort, horse elder, scabwort, yellow starwort, and velvet dock.

The list is long, doubtless because some were found in one month, some in another, some in one locality but not in another.

The white root bark of the hop tree, *Ptelea trifoliata*, was a seasoner that also made a medicine more potent. The trunk bark of black locust, *Robinia pseudacacia*, flavored wild medicines for some Indian tribes, but the white people would have nothing to do with the bark, saying it was poisonous.

The root or berries of the western red raspberry, *Rubus idaeus* var. *aculeatissimus*, made a medicine more palatable. Certainly the berries ought to taste better than the root no matter how you look at it. The root of yellow pimpernel, *Taenidia integerrima*, seemed to help, as did the inner bark of eastern arborvitae, *Thuja occidentalis*.

225

Western mountain ash
Sorbus scopulina

Fennel, *Foeniculum vulgare*, and coriander, *Coriandrum sativum*, were both added to other medicines as a flavoring agent. Lacking either, one could add a little juice of lime, *Succus citri*, if limes were available. Limes grew in the southern states but it was hard indeed to find them growing on the northern plains. These had no medicinal value in themselves, but they could make other medicines more agreeable.

It was believed that ginseng root could be ground and added to other medicines to make any mixture more powerful, but ginseng, *Panax quinquefolium*, had more legendary power than actual medicinal value.

Some Indian tribes made an all-purpose medicine by mixing tendrils of frost grape, *Vitis vulpina*; heads of purple giant hyssop, *Agastache scrophulariaefolia*; leaves of spotted St.-John's-wort, *Hypericum punctatum*; and leaves of willow, *Salix candida*, stewing all together like Macbeth's witches' brew. One hesitates to imagine the taste of such a mixture.

Say you are making such a stew of several varieties of plants for one reason or another. To make it especially effective you must find the inner bark of either the American filbert or hazelnut, *Corylus americana*, or the beaked filbert, *C. cornuta*, and boil that bark with the other herbs. The filbert bark will act as a binder to cement the virtues of all together.

The fruit of the American mountain ash, *Pyrus americana*, was a part of homeopathic remedies, the theory of which was that disease is cured by remedies which produce on a healthy person effects similar to the symptoms of the complaint of the patient. The tree is known by many common names — roundtree, roundwood, American rowan tree, American service tree, mountain sumac, dogberry, quickbeam, wild ash, winetree, witchwood, life-of-man, Indian mozemize, missey-moosey, or moose-misse. In western states the *Pyrus acopulina* is very similar.

Prickly ash, *Zanthoxylum americanum*, was valued in several ways for many medicines, combined or alone. Indeed it seems to have been another of those all-purpose remedies that may have been kept handy at all times. The shrub is known by other names—northern prickly ash, toothache tree, toothache bush, yellowwood, angelica tree, pellitory bark, and suterberry. Prickly ash tea was believed to attack illnesses in the liver, be a general stimulant, and so on.

You could also make an inner bark tea from the white spruce, *Picea glauca*, for those inward troubles.

Goldenseal, *Hydrastis canadensis*, was another plant of many medicines, so much so that its wild growth has been almost exterminated and the plant is grown commercially for easier harvesting. Its rootstock and its leaves, both collected in late summer or autumn, make a fairly good tonic when treated properly, though it is definitely a nonedible plant.

227

TONICS FOR NERVOUSNESS
AND BAD DREAMS

Times change, but human nature does not. Bad dreams are as great a bother today as they always were, and nervousness is as prevalent over the land as when buffaloes were roaming the prairies. The only difference is the treatment.

Where we might take an aspirin for lack of anything better (did someone say an aspirin has nothing to do with nervousness?) the early Americans on the plains country got out the old smoke-saturated blanket and built a fire, throwing on it either a few boughs of the old magic, red cedar, *Juniperus virginiana*, or the root of bush morning-glory, *Ipomoea leptophylla*. Then they inhaled. One wonders if there was not some sort of sedative in the root of that bush morning-glory, because it treated pains of various sorts too.

A simpler remedy to drive fear and nightmares from your sleep was to chew the root of the giant ragweed, *Ambrosia trifida*, before going to bed. It should be easy to find. In wet areas it grows as high as fifteen feet, a giant of a ragweed for sure.

Catnip, *Nepeta cataria*, made a leaf tea that was especially good for children. Though known familiarly as catmint, catwort, or catrup, it was said to allay hysteria arising from nervousness or bad dreams even when it did not actually put one to sleep.

You could gather the root of the hops, *Humulus* spp., for another. Even today the hop is known as a sedative.

Bad dreams are one thing, but if you cannot sleep at all that's worse. That's the time to try partridgeberry, *Mitchella repens*. Menomini Indians in Wisconsin called it the stinking berry but even the whites recognized it as a minor drug. If you want partridgeberry tea, steep the leaves. Other names were twinberry, hive vine, squaw vine, deerberry, foxberry, boxberry, partridge vine, winter clover, chickenberry, cowberry, pigeonberry, snakeberry, teaberry, two-eyed berry, and squaw plum.

Pink lady's-slipper, *Cypripedium acaule*, as a tea brewed from the roots, was a sleep-inducing medicine a century ago. The pink lady's-slipper is hard to find sometimes, and would lose its life in the process of becoming medicine.

228

Pink lady's slipper
Cypripedium acaule

We recommend strongly that you leave the pink lady's-slipper to enhance the bogs where you might find it and drink one of the other teas for your nerves.

A gentle tonic for the nerves was said to be that made from the small yellow lady's-slipper, *Cypripedium calceolus* var. *parviflorum*, a root brew also recognized as a stimulant; or from the showy lady's-slipper, *Cypripedium reginae*, which is even called nerveroot besides ducks and whippoorwill's-shoe.

A plant tea made from the dye bedstraw or small cleavers, *Galium tinctorium*, soothed the nerves; and another was that from the leaves of prickly lettuce, *Lactuca serriola*, or blue lettuce, *L. biennis*.

229

The Virginia bugleweed, *Lycopus virginicus*, has mildly narcotic and astringent properties which would have made it a good nerve tonic. The plant is known by many names—bugleweed, buglewort, sweet bugleweed, American water horehound, carpenter's herb, green archangel, gypsyweed, wolf foot, purple archangel, water bugle, gypsywort, gypsy herb, and Virginia horehound.

The crushed leaves of balm, *Melissa officinalis*, in hot water were good for the nerves as well as a flavoring in foods. Bark tea brewed from chokecherry, *Prunus virginiana*, had a sedative quality besides being good for a host of ailments.

Did you ever hear of tansy tea? Once you know the tansy, *Tanacetum vulgare*, you will never forget it. Tansy's bright-yellow buttons of flowers cover some roadsides completely, fill vacant fields, catch a footing wherever there is room to grow. Along toward late summer we welcome its sunshine for more than one reason. A tansy tea can be brewed from either fresh or dried crushed leaves, and is believed to have a calming effect upon the nerves.

There is an old ghost mining town in the upper reaches of the Black Hills of South Dakota called Carbonate Camp. Most of the buildings are gone from the site of the town but over all the vacant spaces we find the tansy growing waist-high, yellow in its buttons, dark green in its foliage. We can hardly walk through it, so thickly does it grow. We asked a friend who lived there when the town was booming if it had always been that profuse.

"No," she said. "Someone brought tansy to Carbonate because it was used in making whiskey. Now nothing is left except the tansy."

There is one more way in which the tansy can calm the nerves. The vivid flower buttons are extremely tenacious of their color, even when dried. If you would have golden dots for your winter bouquets, pick the tansy flowers without leaves, tie in small bunches, and hang in a shady place to dry. They will keep their color for you all winter long. If beauty will calm your nerves, there it is.

If you feel just generally low and melancholy, try a root tea from the anemones, *Anemone* spp. Some people ridiculed the anemone as not much good, others said it was very valuable.

The candle anemone or long-fruited anemone, *Anemone cylindrica*, was even thought to be beneficial in mending "crazy people."[1]

White settlers have called the root of skunk cabbage, *Symplocarpus foetidus*, both a stimulant for the body and a narcotic to quiet jaded nerves. A general mild stimulant good for children is that made from the extracted oil of garlic, *Allium sativum*. Horse gentian, *Triosteum perfoliatum*, provided a root tea drunk to quiet hysteria or hypochondria. In other words, if you were just generally upset over nothing you should drink horse gentian tea. In spite of its calming effect, one of its popular names was wild coffee.

The root of valerian, *Valeriana* spp., was steeped for a mild sedation against nervous disorders such as hysteria, delirium from exhausting illnesses, nervousness during menopause, or just plain "disorders of the head."[2] Too large a dose can cause mental stupor.

The snowball tree, *Viburnum opulus*, was once thought to control hysteria and calm one to a normal state. The dried inner bark was gathered and a brew was boiled which one gave to the patient.

Two skullcaps were plucked for nervous disorders. The side-flowering skullcap, *Scutellaria lateriflora*, known as mad dog skullcap, madweed, hoodwort, or mad dog, was a general nerve tonic for St. Vitus' dance, convulsions, fits, delirium tremens, or whatever nervous affections appeared. The small skullcap, *Scutellaria parvula*, lent itself particularly to treating St. Vitus' dance, epileptic fits, and nervous exhaustion, but also for other unrelated ailments.

The berries of horse nettle, *Solanum carolinense*, were believed to be good for epilepsy, too. One dried the ripe fruit and boiled them in a concoction that wasn't always safe. Animals eating horse nettle berries have sometimes been poisoned, and that epilepsy treatment could be equally dangerous.

Black sanicle, black snakeroot, *Sanicula marilandica*, was said

---

[1]Huron H. Smith, *Ethnobotany of the Meskwaki Indians*. Bulletin of the Public Museum of the City of Milwaukee, Vol. 4, No. 2. Milwaukee, Wisconsin, April 7, 1928. p. 238.
[2]Smith, *Ethnobotany of the Menomini Indians*, Bulletin of the Public Museum of the City of Milwaukee, Vol. 4, No. 1. Milwaukee, Wisconsin: Dec. 10, 1923. p. 57.

Horse gentian
Triosteum perfoliatum

to yield a root tea of value for such nervous affections as St. Vitus's dance.

You can always chew the root of ginseng, *Panax quinquefolium*, once believed to have qualities to settle the nerves. It might not help, but it wouldn't hurt either.

One that might be dangerous would be the dried pasque-flower, *Anemone patens*, said to be a sedative. The trouble with this is that it might be such a sedative that it would cause the sick one to collapse completely. Doubtless a better sedative would be the cohosh bugbane, *Cimicifuga racemosa*, from which you want the dried rhizome and roots. The dried bark of black haw, *Viburnum prunifolium*, was recognized as a nerve medicine too.

If one was really desperate he could gather some poisonous *Aconitum napellus*, monkshood or wolfsbane, It was said that the dried tuberous roots were a nerve sedative, but since the roots would produce a numbness and tingling when applied to the tongue or lips it is questionable whether the plant would make one more or less nervous.

A small amount of the dried roots of *Baptisia tinctoria*, yellow wild indigo, was apparently safe to take as a nerve stimulant, but again one was warned against taking too much.

Hemp, *Cannabis sativa*, may have been prized for its fibers, but its dried flowering tops were salvaged as a painkiller and a nerve stimulant. This is the plant misused by drug addicts as marijuana or hashish. It has been prepared for medical brews even by recent pharmacists, as a narcotic or cerebral stimulating drug, but it is known in the medical profession as so unstable that other drugs are far preferred for prescriptions. Nevertheless its mind-bending properties were known to primitive people.

It is rather amazing how many of the known poisonous plants were thought to be nerve sedatives. Another was the bittersweet or woody nightshade, *Solanum dulcamara*, the dried stems and branches of which were considered to be a sedative in spite of their poisonous properties.

One notes with relief that common old corn silk from the corn in the field, *Zea mays*, was treated as a mild painkiller in the old days. The farmer's wife gathered the fresh styles and stigmas, the corn silk, and steeped them as medicine.

233

POISONOUS PLANTS

*I*f you have read this far, the chances are even that you might just be curious enough to go into the woods or the meadows to see what is there. We owe a warning to you. Beware! Some plants have one prime purpose in being, to trap you! They're poison. They're beautiful . . . flamboyant in color, tall and stately or cozy and small . . . but some of them are in the same families of plants that are edible or medically valuable, and they *look alike*!

What about poison ivy? Can you positively identify it? This is a climbing vine sometimes shrublike in form. It has glossy green leaves in the summer, turning to a brilliant red in the autumn. What a temptation to bring it into a home for decoration! Don't do it! That poison ivy, *Rhus radicans*, will cause an itching rash on your skin that will drive you to distraction. Here is its sneaky part — it can look like the bright Virginia creeper also known as woodbine, American ivy, or false grape, *Parthenocissus quinquefolia*. The Virginia creeper is perfectly harmless and just as cheery a note in the autumn, but an old Omaha-Ponca name for it translated to "ghost grapes," and that Indian tribe avoided it. There is a difference between the two. The Virginia creeper has five leaflets grouped together and the poison ivy has three leaflets. The Virginia creeper has berries that are dark or blackish in color when ripe; the poison

Poison ivy
Rhus radicans var. *rydbergii*

ivy berries are dun colored or whitish. Both have greenish-white flowers, so look twice to be sure.

The poison ivy growing as a vine, *Rhus radicans*, is known by several names. Call it climbing ivy, three-leaved ivy, poison oak, climath, trailing sumac, climbing sumac, mercury, black mercury vine, markry, markweed, or picry — it is still poison ivy. The low shrub, *Rhus radicans* var. *rydbergi*, is differentiated as western poison ivy, but it is for practical purposes the same devilish plant. In the chapter on skin treatment we have mentioned some of the plants to combat poison ivy itching, but we might also say here that there are a number of standard external remedies on the market today against ivy poisoning. They include ferric chloride, sugar of lead, fluid extract of *Grindelia*, baking soda solution, Epsom salts solution, and carbolated calomine.

In the same breath with poison ivy we may speak of poison oak and poison sumac. The poison oak is a climbing vine or a bushy shrub much like the poison ivy and sometimes lumped with the poison ivy in the botanical appelation *Rhus toxicodendron*. It acts like the ivy, too, with the same disastrous effect upon one's skin. The difference is in the shape of its leaves, which resemble oak leaves to a certain extent. The poison oak is three-leaved in the same manner as the ivy, and poison oak is not a tree. You can find this one and avoid it without too much trouble.

The poison sumac, *Rhus vernix*, is another one that can give a person uneasy moments. It has been called more vicious than poison ivy. The poison sumac is like the other sumacs in its leaves and general build. Its foliage is as beautifully red in the autumn. You can tell its danger easily if you know that the poison sumac has white berries while all the other sumacs have red or purplish berries. Do not gather the autumn leaves of the poison sumac, but any other sumac is all right. Another danger signal lies in the fact that the poison sumac, also known as swamp sumac, poison tree, or poison wood, grows in swampy places. The others like dry ground.

Are you looking for wild grapes? The moonseed, *Menispermum canadense*, can fool you if you don't watch out. Its berries are bluish black with a bloom at the same time the grapes are ripe, but the poisonous moonseed berries have a shape resembling a crescent or a modified horseshoe. Both are climbing vines, but watch the shape of those berries! Early Indian tribes called them "thunder grapes," "grapes of the ghosts," "sore mouth," and "ghost fruit," and avoided them assiduously. The leaves are somewhat different, but you must be alert.

We've talked considerably about the wild onion. We have eaten the bulbs in the spring, added the green upper stalks in salads, suggested them for yellow dye and for cold treatment. Now we must admit with a shudder that there are other bulbous flowers that can fool the novice into thinking they are wild onions. Cattle and sheep have been known to die after eating them. These are the death camass or poison camass, *Zygadenus* spp., and the fly poison or poison lily, *Amianthium muscaetoxicum*, also called hellebore or crow poison.

Remember that there is a camass that can be eaten and was eaten with great relish by Indians and settlers on the frontiers. Called variously the Atlantic camass, midland camass lily, wild hyacinth, eastern camass, or squills, *Camassia scilloides*, or a larger species in the Northwest called camass, *C. quamash*, this can be distinguished from its poisonous cousin because the flowers of the edible camass are blue, and those of the death camass are white. That much must be remembered.

But — and this is important — can you tell the difference between the wild onion, the camass, and the poison lily? All have grasslike leaves. All can have white or whitish flowers, though the wild onion is just as likely to have pink or rosy flowers while the camass in its edible state is blue-flowered. The differences are slight, but important. The wild onion blossoms in a terminal umbel, a pretty little ball of flowers at the top of its stem. The camass flowers are in a loose raceme at the height of its stalk. The poison lily blossoms in a cylindrical group much like the camass but tighter and more compact, and the color of the blossoms changes to a bronzy green after its new whiteness. Moreover, the grasslike leaves of the poison lily are inclined to be blunt-tipped.

We mentioned the sweetroot or sweet cicely, *Osmorhiza longistylis*, suggesting that its roots were pounded to make a poultice for boils or wounds and even eaten by those who knew the anise taste that they held, but we have cautioned

Death camass
Zygadenus sp.
(photograph: Marjorie Morcom)

237

Water hemlock
Cicuta maculata

from the first that the sweet cicely can be mistaken for the deadly poison hemlock, *Conium maculatum*, or for the equally poisonous water hemlock, *Cicuta maculata*. The big cow parsnip, *Heracleum lanatum*, which gave its roots for a medicinal concoction for intestinal pains or a poultice for boils, is a similar plant, tall and flat-topped with white tiny flower clusters. The cow parsnip has enormous leaves. Their size announces immediately that they are not the poison or water hemlocks, although the cow parsnip likes to be near water as well as the water hemlock.

Poison hemlock has myriad names, according to what part of the country you know. It has been called spotted parsley, spotted cowbane, poison parsley, St. Bennet's herb, bad man's oatmeal, wade whistle, cashes, bunk, heck-how, poison root, spotted hemlock, spotted conium, poison snakeweed, and beaver poison.

The water hemlock's common names interlock in some cases, also being called the spotted hemlock, spotted water hemlock, spotted cowbane, beaver poison, children's-bane, musquash poison, and snakeweed.

All four of these plants grow tall with small white clustered flowers at the top of their slender stems, but a mistake can be fatal. A group of Boy Scouts at camp made the error of picking the hollow stems of the water hemlock to use as drinking straws with their milk. They did not die, but they were mighty sick boys. One should know these plants and know them well.

Perhaps the best way to tell these four plants apart is by knowing and recognizing their leaf patterns. The cow parsnip, *Heracleum lanatum*, has those huge elephantine leaves sometimes a foot long and eight inches wide—leaves that you can't miss recognizing. In contrast, the water hemlock, *Cicuta maculata*, has sharp little daggers of leaves about three inches long, several of the leaves growing from one branch extending from the main stalk. The poison hemlock, *Conium maculatum*, has compound leaves with the leaflets cut in a fern pattern, though the leaflets themselves are blunter than the water hemlock and perhaps slightly more jagged-edged. The one that is apt to give the amateur botanist trouble is the sweet cicely, *Osmorhiza longistylis*, because its leaves so closely resemble the poison hemlock. There are differences between the two that may help. The *Range Plant Handbook* issued by the United States Forest Service tells us that the sweet cicely can be readily recognized by its club-shaped seeds, but that will not help if the plant is not in seed stage. The leaves may look alike individually, but the poison hemlock leaves form that fernlike grouping of small leaflets, and the sweet cicely leaves can be said to stand more alone.

If you are not positively sure of these four, leave them all strictly alone. Socrates died from one of them.

The blue lupine that is such a bright splash of color on a hillside is known to be poisonous to sheep or cattle which eat them, but people in an earlier day fed it to their livestock, believing it to be nutritious if eaten before the seeds matured. Particularly for horses, lupine plants were regarded as a fine food. Since human beings do not eat lupines and they are not dangerous when merely handled, this is not too important a

239

warning. Nevertheless you should know that the lupines, *Lupinus* spp., do have a poisonous substance in them when eaten. The lupines have that inconvenient resemblance to another plant that was a blue dye, the *Baptisia australis* or blue wild indigo. The blue wild indigo's leaflets are grouped in threes; the lupine is palmately divided into five to seven or nine leaflets to make a graceful whorl. There's the obvious difference. It is not beyond comprehension that on a lazy afternoon you might be picnicking in the woods, reach a hand for the nearest lupine, and unthinkingly chew on the stem. Don't do it. There are better things to eat.

Old histories tell us that one of the grasses, switch grass, *Panicum virgatum*, is to be avoided when "cutting buffalo meat"[1] because spikelets of the grass stick to the meat and afterward in the throat when eating the meat. This is a mere precautionary word to modern-day hunters who may not cut their game on the prairie but must still clean the animal's intestines from the abdominal cavity before carting the game home. Switch grass can be avoided. although it grows across the plains states on flood plains and valleys, and occasionally in dry rocky soil. Watch for spikelets with smooth sheaths, stems three to five feet high. It has been called panic grass, wild redtop, thatch grass, wobsqua grass, and blackbent.

One of the most startling in its color for autumn bouquets is the scarlet orange-hued bittersweet, *Celastrus scandens*, great armfuls of which are brought into homes for winter decoration. There seems to be some disagreement about whether or not the bittersweet berries are poisonous. As far as we can find out, the whole thing hinges on the fact that there are two plants called bittersweet, and the two are confused by their identical name.

The bittersweet, *Celastrus scandens*, is a staff tree sometimes called false bittersweet, climbing bittersweet, shrubby bittersweet, fevertwig, fevertwitch, staff tree, climbing staff tree, staff vine, waxwork, Roxbury waxwork, yellowroot, and climbing orangeroot. The other, while it is known simply as bittersweet in some localities, is also recognized as woody nightshade,

[1]Melvin R. Gilmore. *Uses of Plants by the Indians of the Missouri River Region.* Bureau of American Ethnology report 1911 – 1912. Washington, D.C.: Government Printing Office, 1919. p. 66.

Lupine
Lupinus sp.

Solanum dulcamara, besides dulcamara, climbing nightshade, amara dulcis, fevertwig, violet-bloom, blue bindweed, felonwort, poisonberry, poison flower, pushion berry, snakeberry, wolf grape, scarletberry, tether-devil, dwale, and skawcoo.

It is said the *Solanum dulcamara* has poisonous or inedible berries. Gilmore says that the Indians living near the Missouri River knew the *Celastrus scandens* had poisonous berries and called the plant snakefood, though H. H. Smith found Wisconsin Indians using them for stomach trouble. In comparing several botanists the weight of the decision shows that *Celastrus* is exceedingly ornamental but not dangerous, while

241

the *Solanum* has berries that may or may not be poisonous but
are certainly inedible. Inasmuch as we have never nibbled
either kind of berry and do not intend to, we merely pass on
the information to you for what it is worth. We do know this
for a fact—the bittersweet, *Celastrus*, will hold its flame-colored
berries long after the leaves have gone from the bare branches,
making it a bright spot of color over the mantelpiece for weeks
after the first snowfall.

We must remind you that the berries and the roots of the
pokeweed, *Phytolacca americana*, are poisonous. We must not
eat them, though we know that Indians and settlers cooked the
young green shoots as a vegetable for many years. Only the
young leafy shoots, if you value your good health. Leave the
berries alone, or if you must gather them for purple dye wash
your hands carefully afterward.

We don't know why it saddens us so much to note that the
pasqueflower or wild crocus (call it by a dozen other names if
you want) is dangerous if taken internally. We do not want to
take it internally, never did, and never will . . . but it has
always meant the freshness of spring to us and we want
nothing to mar its perfection. The crushed leaves have been a
counterirritant for rheumatic aches and pains, though one can
gather the modest lavender crocus in basketfuls and never
have anything more than a sense of peace and well-being.

There are a few flowers which are showy in their coloring
and beautiful in their forms which should be mentioned because of the danger inherent in them. One is snow-on-the-
mountain, *Euphorbia marginata*, that conspicuously white-
topped group of greenish leaves and bracts edged in white that
one can see along roads in foothills areas. The name is mislead-
ing in the northern midwest because the plant is not found in
the mountains but rather on prairies, plains, and waste places
of the flatlands. It is also known as white-margined spurge,
variegated spurge, and mountain snow. The plant is poisonous
in spite of its beauty. Its milky sap causes a skin irritation, and
it should not be eaten.

Who doesn't know the purple larkspurs, *Delphinium* spp.?
They grow on plains and hillsides from one side of the United
States to the other, particularly in the midwestern states. Their
gay banner of deep blue or purple darkens the little gullies or

Snow-on-the-mountain
Euphorbia marginata

243

Snow-on-the-mountain
Euphorbia marginata

shades the meadows with beauty. Once long ago the flower
was called *pied d'alouette* by the French, and lark's-claws or
lark's-heel, all names referring to the spur-shaped projection at
the back of the flowers. One can pick the larkspur in perfect
safety, but it is known to be innately poisonous to cattle and
sheep, horses or mules — any animal that might eat them.
Humans have never been tempted to eat the larkspur but they
have graced many a table as a centerpiece. If one knows the
hidden danger we may still enjoy the larkspur.

A cousin of the larkspur is the monkshood, *Aconitum* spp.,

244

that strange and striking purple flower that suggests a monk's cowl over a hidden face. These, too, are harmless to handle but are violent poison if eaten. The plants have been part of old medicines, and the drug aconite is obtained from the roots today, but if the plant is mistakenly eaten it can be fatal. Best to let the monkshood grow unmolested.

Rattleweed or rattlebox is another one poisonous for animals. This one can blossom in yellow, blue, violet, or variegated colors, and is beaked in form to give its name. The Greek *rhinos*, "nose," and *anthos*, "flower," combine to describe it with the word *Rhinanthus*. In the western hills we are most familiar with *Rhinanthus kyrollae*, or yellow rattle.

Do not forget the jimsonweed or thorn apple, *Datura stramonium*. This funnel-shaped white- or violet-flowered plant can grow from two to four feet high, and its blossoms have been found as large as eight inches long, though most of them are smaller. It is ill-smelling, but that is a virtue if it will keep you away from the jimsonweed. The plant is dangerously poisonous and narcotic. For years it grew principally east of the Mississippi River but now one finds it on the western banks too. It is said to cause delirium for days if one eats parts of it. The plant has many names, including Jamestown weed, Jamestown lily, devil's-apple, mad apple, stinkweed, stinkwort, devil's trumpet, and dewtry.

Though a few of the many species of *Astragalus* found on the prairie lands were known as medicines in frontier days, the common or popular name for *Astragalus* is still the locoweed. Briefly, many species of *Astragalus* contain a poison that affects cattle. They become afflicted with a sort of insanity, a slow poisoning that can cause death within a period of months or even a year or two. One of the most dangerous is the woolly locoweed, rattleweed, crazyweed, or rattlebag weed, *Astragalus mollissimus*.

The blossoms of *Astragalus* species can be white, lavender, red, or yellow, and some of them are truly a sight to see. They can be handled with impunity, but keep them out of your mouth and keep the cattle from grazing on them. One of the prettiest in our estimation is the white orophaca, *Astragalus gilviflorus*, though the purple or lavender blossoms of other species are as eye-catching. Many of these plants were ancient

Locoweed
Oxytropis sp.

rattleweeds for ceremonial occasions. The dry pods can be lifted with the stalks to make a satisfactory noisemaker.

Also called locoweed or crazyweed as well as stemless loco and rattleweed was the related Lambert's crazyweed, *Oxytropis lamberti*. Known to be a poisonous forage plant, it is nevertheless eaten by hungry livestock with about the same results as *Astragalus* locoweeds.

We found a few plants recognized as antidotes for poison taken internally.

The root of the roundhead lespedeza was one. This plant, *Lespedeza capitata*, is known as roundhead bush clover, rabbit

Locoweed
Astragalus hypoglottis

foot, or just bush clover. A root extract could be made from the root of Allegheny blackberry, *Rubus allegheniensis*, to drink as a poison antidote; or the root of the great dock, *Rumex orbiculatus*, sometimes called great water dock or horse sorrel, was boiled.

Another antidote is a brew from the root of the butterfly weed, *Asclepias tuberosa*. It is known to be effective in causing vomiting as well as a strong laxative when taken in large doses, and perhaps its purging action is the valuable effect in combatting poison.

Three milkweeds are listed as potentially poisonous plants, particularly when found growing in selenium soil, including the poison milkweed, *Asclepias galioides*; the Mexican milkweed, *A. fascicularis*; and the whorled milkweed, *A. verticillata*, the poisonous principle being a resinous substance soluble in alcohol.

The sneezeweed, *Helenium autumnale*, prescribed in combatting colds, is very poor forage for cattle to the point of being called poisonous too.

As a matter of fact, Walter Conrad Muenscher in his *Poisonous Plants of the United States* lists ninety-eight plants causing dermatitis depending on the susceptibility of the individual, and discusses about four hundred species of poisonous plants which affect edibility to livestock or humans, skin irritation of humans, or mechanical harm such as might occur from cactus. Many of these are of only slight danger or are primarily dangerous to livestock which eat them. For the most part all we need is to know the dangers in those plants which may be toxic. Recognize their idiosyncrasies of form and color as a commonsense measure, and we can still walk through the woods and the meadows and enjoy every moment of our stroll. The bright cradles of color of these flowers add their beauty to the forests and the grasslands, and if we know them we can welcome them as we do their quieter friends.

BIBLIOGRAPHY

Armstrong, Margaret. *Field Book of Western Wild Flowers*. New York: G. P. Putnam, 1915.

Armstrong, Moses K. *The Early Empire Builders of the Great West*. 1866. Reprinted, St. Paul, Minn.: E. W. Porter, 1901.

Bakeless, John. *The Eyes of Discovery*. Philadelphia: Lippincott, 1950.

Barr, Claude. *Native Plants from the High Plains, Badlands and Black Hills*. South Dakota: privately printed, 1954.

Brackenridge, H. M. *Journal of a Voyage up the River Missouri, 1816*. Baltimore: 1815. Reprinted in Reuben Gold Thwaites, *Early Western Travels* (Cleveland: Arthur H. Clark Co., 1904).

Bradbury, John. *Travels in the Interior of America, 1809 – 1811*. London: 1819. Reprinted in Reuben Gold Thwaites, *Early Western Travels* (Cleveland: Arthur H. Clark Co., 1904).

Breck, Joseph. *New Book of Flowers*. New York: Orange Judd and Co., 1866.

Britton, Nathaniel Lord, and Brown, Hon. Addison. *Illustrated Flora of the Northern United States, Canada and the British Possessions*. New York: Scribner's, 1913.

Chittenden, Hiram Martin. *American Fur Trade of the Far West*. New York: Press of the Pioneers, 1935.

Clements, Frederic E., and Clements, Edith S. *Rocky Mountain Flowers*. New York: H. W. Wilson Co., 1914; reprinted, 1945.

Colliers Encyclopedia, P. F. Collier and Son. New York: 1954.

BIBLIOGRAPHY

Dana, Mrs. William Starr. *How to Know the Wild Flowers*. New York: Scribner's, 1899.

Dayton, William A. *Notes on Western Range Forbs*. Washington, D.C.: Forest Service, U.S. Department of Agriculture, 1960.

Encyclopedia Americana, 1949. New York: Americana Corporation, 1949.

Encyclopedia Britannica, 1953. London: 1953.

Fernald, M. L. *Gray's Manual of Botany*, 8th edition. New York: American Book Co., 1950.

Forest Service, U.S. Department of Agriculture. *Range Plant Handbook*. Washington, D.C.: Government Printing Office, 1937.

Gilmore, Melvin R. *Indian Lore and Indian Gardens*. Ithaca, N.Y.: Slengerland-Comstock Co., 1930.

Gilmore, Melvin R. *Plant Relations in North Dakota*. Grand Forks, N.D.: University of North Dakota, 1921.

Gilmore, Melvin R. *Uses of Plants by the Indians of the Missouri River Region*. Bureau of American Ethnology report 1911 – 1912. Washington, D.C.: Government Printing Office, 1919.

Gleason, Henry A. *The New Britton and Brown Illustrated Flora of the United States and Canada*. Lancaster, Pa.: Lancaster Press, Inc., 1952.

Gottscho, Samuel. *Pocket Guide to the Wildflowers*. New York: Pocket Books, 1951.

Gray, Asa. *Botany of the Northern United States*, 1889.

Gray, Asa. *Lessons in Botany and Vegetable Physiology*. New York and Chicago: Ivison, Blakeman, Taylor & Co., 1873.

Gray, Asa. *New Manual of Botany*, 7th edition. New York: American Book Co., 1908.

Harrington, H. D. *Manual of the Plants of Colorado*. Denver: Sage Books, 1954.

House, Homer D. *Wild Flowers*. New York: Macmillan, 1942.

Irving, Washington. *Captain Bonneville*. New York: Collier, 1868.

Kelsey, Harlan, and Dayton, William A. *Standardized Plant Names*. American Joint Committee on Horticultural Nomenclature. Harrisburg, Pa.: J. Horace McFarland Co., 1942.

Kohman, Edward F. "The Chemical Components of Onion Vapors Responsible for Wound Healing Qualities," *Science Magazine*, Dec. 26, 1947. Baltimore: American Association for the Advancement of Science.

Larpenteur, Charles. *Forty Years a Fur Trader*. New York: Harper, 1898.

Lee County Columbian Club. *Recollections of the Pioneers of Lee County*. Dixon, Ill.: Inez A. Kennedy, 1893.

Lewis and Clark. *Original Journals of the Lewis and Clark Expedition*, edited by Reuben Gold Thwaites. New York: Dodd, Mead & Co., 1904.

MacIntosh, Arthur C. *A Botanical Survey of the Black Hills of South Dakota*. Rapid City, S.D.: South Dakota State School of Mines, May 1931.

Matthews, F. Schuyler. *Field Book of American Wild Flowers*. New York: G. P. Putnam, 1927.

Maximilian, Prince of Wied. *Travels in the Interior of North America*. Reprinted in Reuben Gold Thwaites, *Early Western Travels* (Cleveland: Arthur H. Clark Co., 1906).

McDougall, W. B., and Baggley, Herma A. *Plants of Yellowstone National Park*. Washington, D.C.: Government Printing Office, 1936.

Medsger, Oliver Perry. *Edible Wild Plants*. New York: Macmillan, 1939.

Miloradovich, Milo. *The Home Garden Book of Herbs and Spices*. Garden City, N.Y.: Doubleday, 1952.

Modern American Encyclopedia. New York: Instructive Books, Inc., 1949.

Muenscher, Walter C. *Poisonous Plants of the United States*. New York: Macmillan, 1939.

Munz, Philip A. *California Spring Wildflowers*. Berkeley and Los Angeles: University of California Press, 1961.

National Geographic Society. *The Book of Wild Flowers*. 1924.

Nelson, Ruth Ashton. *Plants of Rocky Mountain National Park*. Washington, D.C.: Government Printing Office, 1953.

Nuttall, Thomas. *Journal of Travels into the Arkansas Territory*. Philadelphia: Thos. H. Palmer Press, 1821. Reprinted in Reuben Gold Thwaites, *Early Western Travels* (Cleveland: Arthur H. Clark Co., 1905).

Over, William H. *Flora of South Dakota*. Vermillion, S.D.: University of South Dakota, 1932.

Over, William H., and Churchill, Edward P. *Mammals of South Dakota*. Vermillion, S.D.: University of South Dakota, 1945.

Pesman, M. Walter. *Meet the Natives*. Denver: Smith Brooks, 1946.

Petry, E. J. *Weeds and Their Control*. Brookings, S.D.: Bulletin #211, South Dakota State College Experiment Station, December 1924.

Platt, Rutherford. *A Pocket Guide to the Trees*. New York: Pocket Books, 1952.

Preston, Richard J. *Rocky Mountain Trees*. Iowa State College Press, 1947.

Randolph, Vance. *Ozark Mountain Folks*. New York: Vanguard, 1932.

Rebbeck, Dick. "Survival Definite Possibility if You Rely on Native Hills Plants," *Rapid City Daily Journal*, Aug. 17, 1960.

Remington, Joseph P., assisted by Cook, E. Fullerton. *The Practice of Pharmacy*, 6th edition. Philadelphia: Lippincott, 1917.

Rickett, H. W. *Wild Flowers of America*. New York: Crown, 1953.

Russell, J. Almus. "Doctoring with Herbs," *Frontiers Magazine*, February 1957. Philadelphia: Academy of Natural Sciences, 1957.

Rydberg, P. A. *Flora of the Rocky Mountains and Adjacent Plains*. New York: the author, 1917.

Sargent, Charles Sprague. *Manual of the Trees of North America*. Boston and New York: Houghton Mifflin, 1905.

Saunders, Charles Francis. *Useful Wild Plants of the United States and Canada*. New York: Robert M. McBride and Co., 1920.

Science Service. "Dreams Still Guide Destiny of Millions," *Rapid City Daily Journal*, Rapid City, S.D., Oct. 14, 1962.

Sievers, A. F. *American Medicinal Plants of Commercial Importance*. Miscellaneous Publication No. 77. Washington, D.C.: U.S. Department of Agriculture, July 1930.

Smith, Huron H. *Ethnobotany of the Menomini Indians*. Bulletin of the Public Museum of the City of Milwaukee, Vol. 4, No. 1. Milwaukee: Dec. 10, 1923.

Smith, Huron H. *Ethnobotany of the Meskwaki Indians*. Bulletin of the Public Museum of the City of Milwaukee, Vol. 4, No. 2. Milwaukee: April 7, 1928.

Smith, Huron H. *Ethnobotany of the Ojibwe Indians*. Bulletin of the Public Museum of the City of Milwaukee, Vol. 4, No. 3. Milwaukee: May 2, 1932.

Standley, Paul C. *Plants of Glacier National Park*. Washington, D.C.: Government Printing Office, 1926.

Swartzlow, Carl R., and Upton, Robert F. *Badlands National Monument, South Dakota*. Natural History Handbook Series No. 2. Washington, D.C.: Government Printing Office, 1957.

Taylor, Norman. *A Guide to the Wild Flowers*. Garden City, N.Y.: Garden City Publishing Co., 1928.

Thwaites, Reuben Gold. *Early Western Travels*. Cleveland: Arthur H. Clark Co., 1904–1905–1906.

"Tiny Ragweed Pollen Creates Major Misery," *Rapid City Daily Journal*, Rapid City, S.D., Aug. 31, 1960.

Townsend, John K. *Narrative of a Journey Across the Rocky Mountains*. Philadelphia: 1839. Reprinted in Reuben Gold Thwaites, *Early Western Travels* (Cleveland: Arthur H. Clark Co., 1905).

The Volume Library. New York: Educational Publishers, 1939.

Webster's Collegiate Dictionary. Springfield, Mass.: C. & C. Merriam Co., 1937.

Wherry, Edgar T. *Wild Flower Guide*. Garden City, N.Y.: Doubleday, 1948.

Zim and Martin. *Flowers*. New York: Simon and Schuster, 1950.

Zim and Martin. *Trees*. New York: Simon and Schuster, 1956.

INDEX

255

258

259